stitched up sue

VOLUME ONE

Inspired by my mother's memoirs, the true events depicted in this story have been partly reimagined and aggrandized using anecdotal tales.

by

MAMTA ANAND SHAD

Copyright © 2023 Mamta Anand Shad

All rights reserved. Without limiting the rights under copyright reserved above, no part of this publication may be reproduced, stored in, or introduced into a retrieval system, or transmitted, in any form, or by any means without the prior written permission of the author.

CONTENTS

AUTHOR'S BACKGROUND v

PREFACE xxi

ACKNOWLEDGEMENT xxix

DEDICATIONS. xxxiii

PROLOGUE xxxix

Chapter 1.   FRACTURED. 1

Chapter 2.   ELEUTHEROMANIA .20

Chapter 3.   FATHER'S REIGN. 31

Chapter 4.   UNANSWERED PRAYERS 43

Chapter 5.   'PROPER GIRL' 50

Chapter 6.   E = MC 2- Squared 68

Chapter 7.   TERE GHAR KE SAMNE
                  (OPPOSITE YOUR HOUSE). 79

Chapter 8.   SHIFTING 90

Chapter 9.   GENESIS 101

Chapter 10. FALLING 118

Chapter 11. LEMONADE 127

Chapter 12. LOVER'S DREAM. 139

Chapter 13. FORBIDDEN FRUIT 156

Chapter 14. PHOENIX. 163

Chapter 15. RUNAWAY 174

Chapter 16. STITCHED UP 194

AUTHOR'S BACKGROUND

I spent many years looking in the wrong direction, searching for inspiration. Mesmerised by the bygone era of Bollywood and the Golden age of Hollywood and its alluring paragon stars; like Vyjayanthi Mala, Madhubhala, Nawab Bano, Nargis, Marlena Dietrich, Marilyn Monroe, Bettie Davis, and Katherine & Audrey Hepburn- I imagined how wonderful it must be having such fame and fortune and being so adored. Most wonderful of all, being able to leave a legacy- immortalising you; long after you're gone. In the simplest sense, it was the epitome of living life- to do something you loved, had a passion and talent for; and from which you could make a living.

Having spent most of my childhood earnestly entertaining guests with impromptu dancing, singing, and mimicked caricatures, it was early on that I stumbled upon my uncanny ability to stand out from the crowd. When people would look at me with intrigue, delight, even shock or disgust, I'd revel in it and want to recreate it repeatedly. Taking every chance to volunteer for demonstrations or perform in school shows, I'd always pitch myself for the most significant parts, and it wasn't long before I was top of Drama class. But it was when aged eleven that, a chanced casting led my unsuspecting sister and me to play extras in Stephen Spielberg's blockbuster movie- 'Indiana Jones & The Temple of Doom'- which determined my fate. Though we were merely two of numerous other indistinguishable, brown-faced kids loitering on set- I felt instantly enthralled by the real world of make belief. Besides the star-studded cast, consisting of such heavyweight actors as Mr. Harrison Ford, the captivating Kate Capshaw, and the infamous, Bollywood villain- Mr. Amrish Poori, it was the very magic of moving pictures, in conjunction with the costumes, make-up, sets, props, and lighting; which felt like being transported, into a whole new world. That ten-week filming stint- cast over my last summer break before starting high school, was the best ever, and with my raging hormones, right on the cusp of puberty, I was alight!

Pursuant to completing High school, with A-stars in Drama and English- when I wasn't chasing the next- 'Mr. Wrong,' I was seeking validation from casting agents and directors instead. This insatiable craving often leading me into perennial situations and in the company of many duplicitous characters, and each time, only starving me further of the very validation I craved.

My first foray into significant acting was partaking in a low-budget, locally filmed Hindi movie called 'Chitti' *(Letter)*, which led to years of performing in Punjabi theatre shows. Plays like- 'Bebe Vilayat Vich' *(Mother-in-Law in London)*, 'Desi Munda, Vilayati Kurri' *(Indian Boy, London Girl)*, and 'Chutkara' *(Release)*- were very popular and well received by the South Asian communities around England and formed a solid training ground for ensemble, live performance techniques. Besides that, I also danced on stage at many 'daytimer gigs' and Bhangra concerts with bands like 'Pardesi,' 'Heera Group' and 'Premi' and compered live entertainment shows at festivals, as well as presented with a variety of local cable T.V. & radio channels like, 'The Community Channel, Zee T.V, Namaste T.V. and Asia Net.' I even dabbled in some small-town modelling and journalism, writing theatre reviews for the local Teletext and in my column- 'Mouthy moments with Mamta!' for the popular entertainment magazine 'Snoop'- whilst doing whatever I could to pursue my big break!

However, it wasn't until the summer of 1990, after being introduced to a music promoter twice my age and married with kids, that things revved up a notch. Well-connected within the fast-emerging, British-Asian music and entertainment scene, his convictions of my promising career and his confident charm offensive; had us all taken in. No sooner was he escorting me to music studios, publicity events, showbiz parties, and expensive restaurants; than he was also showing me off as his newly discovered prodigy. Suddenly, I found myself on the front covers of Asian entertainment magazines and a new Bhangra music album. One Saturday morning, he even drove me around to surprise me with my posters- plastered over billboards and at bus stops all over town! Designer clothes and expensive jewellery gifts quickly followed this flattery before he went on to introduce me to other wealthy, famous, and influential people. Effectively placing me upon a pedestal and treating me like a fully-fledged star, he'd fed ideally into my voided centre. Besides this, playing grown-up with the grown-ups and stardom with the stars was also fun! What more could a naive and impressionable 16-year-old girl from Southall want? You might wonder. But I'd failed to realise then that I was systematically being groomed! One night-while on an album launch in Blackburn, things came to a head (so to speak!) - after he'd arranged for us to share a room and a bed! - claiming that "...there were no more rooms at the inn!" In the middle of the night, he was suddenly propositioning me, not least with physical advances but also a shocking declaration of love! Left bewildered, confused, and afraid of upsetting him, I spent the next few hours completely frozen to the edge of the bed and with one eye- left wide open for the rest of the night! The last time, I felt so incredibly vulnerable and helpless; I was eight years old and sexually molested by a trusted family friend and religious elder in our community.

Days on, when my former naive flirtations (which were simply part of my vivacious personality- whether in the company of males, females, or even felines!) failed to transpire into a complete submission for sex- I quickly realised he was not such a sweet uncleji, after all! Casually informing me that- '... I'd be expected to *compromise* and *adjust* (as he liked to put it!) not only with him but with his entourage, too!' he'd even suggested- 'I learned to dangle the carrot with men' and merely promise sexual favours, without the full delivery of my vagina! One such man was a wealthy Bollywood movie producer- old enough to be my Granddad! Who'd offered me the starring role in his next big-budget horror movie- on the proviso that I *compromised* with him, of course!

"Mamta darling... all the stars, compromise and adjust. This is just Show-business! Besides, you are young and beautiful- why not use it?" He eagerly placated me with idol flattery, impervious to my disgust!

"But I can make it on my own merit. I actually have- talent!" I vainly tried convincing him.

No sooner had I pulled the drawbridge up that the novelty of this perceived stardom was fast wearing off, and my rose-tinted glasses were clearing in vision. Revealing the true nature of the beast, I realised that most of the leachy older men surrounding me- I'd assumed as reverent and benevolent; were predators and opportunistic vultures looking for their next feed! Some were compensating for their scorned 'little man' egos! While others wanted to claim a slice of my still-virgin pie! With this sobering realisation came the first of many lifelong lessons- 'When something seems too good to be true- it usually is!' And 'Nothing that comes easy; ever lasts!'

Feet, firmly back on the ground and pride, a little battered; at least I was a little wiser when I enrolled on the 4 A-level course- FEDAS (Film, English, Drama and Art Studies) at Hounslow Borough College and hoped to attain greater knowledge and expertise in my craft, to navigate a more credible route towards my dreams. I read numerous acting theory books and subscribed to 'The Stage, Melody Maker and Spotlight'- while continually scouring weekly audition pages and turning up for any auditions- even when blatantly obvious- that the other beaming wannabes surrounding me were better fits for the job. Most seemed to be far more talented, knowledgeable, experienced, and beautiful than me, often landing the parts over me.

Finally, I'd come to accept; I'd never be that size zero heroine I longed to be. Let alone that accomplished classical dancer or skilled jazz singer! (The likes of whom I'd fooled myself into competing with!) These accomplished rivals possessed many years of gruelling stage school training. They'd honed their skills and techniques via expensive private tutors as if perfectly manufactured for their cause. Arriving at auditions like they'd skipped straight out of Italia Conti and wearing skin-tight leotards, they'd flick their silky blonde ponytails and size three ballet shoes from their swan-like necks. At the same time, I'd turn up looking more like the local village tramp! With my frizzy wild hair, micro mini-skirts, and kinky boots and stomp about the place with the comparative grace of a baby hippo! Barely able to reach the musical notes, let alone my toes! These girls were a different breed and another class altogether. Most came from wealthier and better-connected families and relied on nepotism to help jump queues- if not network their way through casting director's doors or straight onto their couch! Others were luckier than me as if the stars were predestined and aligned for their success. But the most notable difference of all; was the mere fact that they were all white! They were the fortunate and privileged few for whom most credible parts were written and whose aryan race image continually saturated and dominated mainstream entertainment.

After finishing college, I took a gap year and my first-ever flight to the States. Working as a Camp counsellor/Drama specialist at a charitable Christian summer camp in New York, I was, again, catapulted into another life-affirming and memorable adventure. Returning three months later with a renewed enthusiasm for performing. Even while having realised, that I was too British for Bollywood and too Brown for Britain! Nonetheless, I sat comfortably in a little niche of the market, performing with touring fringe theatre companies and in T.I.E. (Theatre in Education) or charity/council-funded community theatre projects, performing in shows like- 'Just So Stories' by Sixth Sense Theatre 'The Honoured Guest' by Twisting Yarn Theatre, 'Unkahi *(Unspoken)*' by Women & Theatre and 'Grandpa's Jīn' by M6 Theatre and 'Rush, Wigga and M.P.H.' by Big Fish Theatre.

I learned the hard graft of sustaining two to three performances at various locations per day and having to facilitate draining workshops alongside, continually jumping in and out of tour buses and vans and repeatedly loading, off-loading, setting up, and dismantling, often mammoth heavy stage sets, against a ticking clock! By now, I'd gotten used to living light-footed and fancy-free, on the bare minimum of luxuries and out of my tattered suitcase as I traipsed across the country, away from home months on end and residing in often unsavoury digs, while performing at often obscure venues. I quickly adopted the life of a vagabond gypsy, caught inside a vacuumed state, forming unusually close bonds with fellow performers and stagehands while becoming part of an adopted family.

However, with each tour's end would also come the end of our short-lived love affairs, when our adopted families would wind up divorced. Returning us to our former lives, we'd all resume our cycles of existence, no sooner replacing those seemingly irreplaceable and unbreakable friendships and waiting for life to hit repeat. When another tour would kick start, alongside another love affair and another make-believe family and our previously tethered lives would untether again. Alas, such was the life of a touring artist. But I was determined- these early years of self-afflicted toil, graft, and hardship would only serve to shape, strengthen, and fortify my spirit, character, and resolve and form part of my signature back story- once I was rich and famous! Following in my idolised predecessor's steps; I'd, too, naively assumed that the grittier the struggle on my road to success; the more deserved and rewarding my claim to fame would be. (While also providing a more exciting read in future memoirs!)

After a few more years, beset with the paucity of opportunities, I started to rely on more self-generated theatre and film projects, once again often orchestrated by a coterie of like-minded British Asian thespians and artists. All of whom were also tired and frustrated by the meaningless bit parts and who also sought to express themselves from the vantage of our shared diaspora. Working towards a more even- playing field, our mutual ambition to create a benefic, solid foundation helped us seek out other artists; who might also inspire and instigate commentary and discussion upon many relevant social and political issues, which stem from the many contradictions of our dual British Asian identity and the juxtaposition of our traditions and culture, against a yearning to fit in with modern British society.

Finally, after being spotted at the Edinburgh Fringe Festival, performing with the comedy troupe- 'The Funjabis,' I was signed up by a professional managing agent and subsequently landed a few more notable yet generic and stereotypical T.V. parts. Most often playing a typical 'Indian Doctor, Nurse, Lawyer, Teacher, or Cornershop owner' in shows like 'Kismet Road,' 'The Bill,' 'Casualty,' 'Doctors,' and 'Fifteen Stories High.' Although these parts were well paid and seemed to impress most of my family and friends, they were sometimes artistically restrictive and tokenistic. Some reinforced negative stereotypes, while others relied on mimicry and mockery or were there to dress the set and fill in for the lead Caucasian character's storyline. Yet, for a jobbing actor- any work was better than none, and I certainly wasn't ready to forgo the career development, training, and networking opportunities each experience offered.

My roles on stage, too, often came with a prerequisite use of a black wig, donning a white badger stripe, alongside a black bin liner style- Indian suit, or else a hijab, effectively shrouding my early 20's figure to assimilate that of a frumpy 40/50-year-old aunty ji! Alongside my well-accomplished Indian accents, natural flare for on-demand tears, sharp comic timing, and finely tuned-cliché mannerisms and dance moves- I'd found myself some small-town success playing; 'The Interfering Aunty, The Over-Protective Mother, The Meddling Mother-In-Law, or Abused Housewife.' In shows like- 'Pleasure & Pain' by Kali Theatre, 'The Cornershop' by Manmella Theatre, 'When Amar Met Jay' by Hungama Theatre 'Bollywood, yet another love story, and 'Deranged Marriage' by Rifco Theatre Company. I also acted in a few films like- 'The King of Bollywood,' 'Whodunnit,' 'Bollywood Sketches,' 'A Quiet Desperation,' 'The Wounded Sky/Restless Skies,' 'Johnathan's Dead' and 'Talking about Suicide.' On the rare occasion when I was cast in my actual age range, I'd always be the demi heroine or the goofy, chubby girlfriend- who was always the bridesmaid but never the bride!

Yet even with the late 1990s and early noughties proving my busiest acting decade, I still battled with ongoing uncertainties, financial insecurity, and emotional upheavals resulting from my career. It was always either; feast or famine, stardom or obscurity, joy or misery, sunshine or showers, and much like my yo-yo-ing waistline, my battle with depression, yoyoed too! Constantly feeling like I was walking a tightrope- where one day, I'd feel like a little star, performing in a sold-out show, receiving standing ovations, and glorifying accolades, and the next- queuing up at a dole office with my pride in my shoes! If I weren't signing autographs at the stage door of a beautiful, Victorian theatre, I'd instead be signing for my social security check in a run-down office block surrounded by junkies! It created an almost bipolar-type existence- whereby the highs were indeed high, but the lows- were just as low! At the time, I had little idea what long-term damage was impacting my health, with this sustained state of nerves and perpetual fight or flight.

Sure enough, The End came even sooner than I could have predicted when an unexpected fall performing on stage triggered a long-term incurable illness called 'Fibromyalgia' (F.M.S.) Causing unexplainable myofascial all-over body pains, migraines/cognitive issues, severe muscle tension/stiffness/strains, insomnia, chronic fatigue, and many other debilitating daily symptoms. Notwithstanding this, I still believed that mind over matter could be my panacea and, along with the misapprehension, that the doctors had got it all wrong. - I still battled onwards, as the proliferation of my symptoms only got worse.

Alas, when I wasn't drying up on stage or forgetting my lines and going blank before the large film and T.V. crews, I'd instead struggle to keep up with the strenuous workout regimes. Lacking the basic stamina to perform well in shows; soon, I even had issues projecting my voice. To the point of being hollered at- live-mid shows, by audiences, telling me to- 'Speak Up!' Suddenly, I'd gone from being praised for my energy, enthusiasm, and first-off script; to being most off my A-game. Receiving the bulk of after-show notes from often perplexed Directors, or bullish choreographers, I was constantly singled out with disparaging critique, being humiliated in front of my peers- doing little to help my already wavering self-esteem! Yet none of them knew how desperate things were behind closed doors. What terrible battles I secretly fought behind my façade. After all, I was an actress and good at hiding behind my big smile, and whether onstage or off, I kept up the show! I couldn't afford to turn down any acting work or show my weaknesses. The irony of it being an invisible illness helped, too, for I could often appear fully functioning and well; while feeling terribly sick and unwell, if not on the verge of imminent death! This illness was not only stripping away my abilities and skills; but also, my sense of identity and self-worth. While simultaneously setting about shattering all my former dreams.

A rare condition at the time, there was little known about Fibromyalgia, and even fewer long-lasting treatment options or medications available. So, for a time; I led a secret double life; barely surviving on prescription painkillers, alcohol, and occasional marijuana joints and always desperately trying to numb the physical and mental pain. I even started wondering *if I was better off dead!* Seeing doctor after doctor and specialist after specialist- I tried all I could to help myself better- from starting drastic elimination diets and living off superfood juicing fasts to forcing myself into exercise regimes and endless relaxation techniques. Yet after a certain point, I'd always wind up feeling the exact onset of symptoms again!

I researched my illness and other similar illnesses- like C.F.S. (chronic fatigue syndrome), M.E. (Myalgia encephalomyelitis), M.S. (Multiple Sclerosis), and Lupus, through medical journals, books, and online forums. But still, the answers were scarce, and the research; limited. With no real cures and barely any help and support available, I was left feeling alone in my battle.

Soon, I came to realise that it was time to stop running and face facts; to accept my new reality and begrudgingly admit- that if I could no longer do the job at hand, for which I was being paid, then like it or not; it was time to quit! Even if, after many years of pushing hard for these dreams, I felt humiliated or felt like I was tumbling back down a giant mountain, having almost just reached the top! It sent me into an even deeper spiral of depression, and I quickly realised that sometimes, letting go of what you want takes more courage than holding on.

Luckily, the many years of networking paid off, and I landed various freelance contracts. Allowing greater flexibility and frequent respite, most still allowed me to utilise my specialist skill set. Taking on many training opportunities and work placements, I was fortunate that the variety of work kept me on my toes and from getting bored. I worked as a Nursery nurse, a private Nanny, a Drama tutor, a supply teacher, a Playscheme Leader, a kids-club Manager, a Youth Worker, a Youth Offender's Facilitator, and a children's Chaperone. I even took kids on holiday, here and abroad, with initiatives like Princes Trust, The Duke of Edinburgh awards, and PGL Paris. Using performance arts to engage often marginalised and disenfranchised youths, I also went on to write and direct various youth theatre shows, like- 'What's It Worth?' (About drug addiction) 'Tuff Love'- (about domestic violence and identity), 'No More Bull'- (about bullying and teenage suicide), and 'R.I.P.'- (about Islamophobia and extremist ideology), all of which were well received, with one even going on to win the acclaimed- Philip Lawrence Award!

But it wasn't until age 30 that I accidentally stumbled across a position within which I felt the greatest affinity and satisfaction. A job that could, at last, parallel my passion for performance. While working as an outreach tutor with the College of Northwest London, I taught key foundation skills, Drama, and communication studies, to adults with complex physical and mental needs. Simultaneously completing my formal teaching degree, through distance learning, with The University of Greenwich- I worked so diligently that I even managed to complete my three-year degree course in just one year!

At the time, most of my students battled various disabilities and chronic illnesses, ranging from Dementia, Schizophrenia, Bipolar, Alzheimer's, Downs Syndrome to Autism and Parkinson's disease. Yet, their enthusiasm for learning and child-like curious intrigue was infectious and inspiring. As if they were staring defiantly into the face of adversity and proclaiming, 'And so what?' On days when my illness compromised my ability to carry on with my work, I'd need only to be in their presence momentarily; to feel a mutual re-alignment take place; while swept on their wanton zest for life and living. With this newly found grace and gratitude, a small light bulb went off inside my head. Fascinated by my student's past stories, I used various storytelling techniques to illicit anecdotal tales; as we explored; individual past lives and considered how life's events, experiences, choices, and decisions- might otherwise inspire, affect, define, validate, influence, and unlock our personalities or inform our future. Our memories became mini mind maps into our lives, and each one could trace our footsteps walked on this earth; each story could one day be recalled in remembrance, celebration, and even to provide comfort to those mourning our loss and like individual fingerprints or blueprints of our lives; our stories, like an essence of us; would be left behind, once we are gone. It was also impossible to deny that almost magical, melancholic allure our shared nostalgia bought us all as we gazed into the past.

In time, we'd found some surprising past lives; amongst many heart-warming tales and discovered some enlightening previous passions, accomplishments, and even careers. Some shared with us; fascinating childhoods seeped in migration stories, distant travels, and witnessing or even partaking in devastating conflicts and wars. Most stories, often harshly juxtaposed with complex family histories and childhoods blighted by trauma and pain, stemmed from shared experiences of cultural bias, ignorance, and stigmas associated with disabilities, ill health, and old age.

While some students were hard to contain- once we'd merely scratched the surface; others required their stories to be gently coaxed out of them. Some shared little jigsaw pieces, like cryptic clues into their pasts. And the remaining few seemed to get confused by what was fictitious and real, with some even plucking tales out of thin air!

Though many stories seemed on their surface, at least, to be tragic and sad tales of being discriminated against and ostracised, once we'd all looked deeper, these same stories started to shift upon an axle. Just as our gaze shifted via our perspective and new point of view and soon, it was as if even the saddest and most mundane story could, in parts, be found to be triumphant, inspiring, and even offer the listener unsuspected nuggets of hope, humour, interest, and joy. Those previously supposed victims and sufferers in a story; might emerge as quiet victors and heroes of their tales; once we've learned how to focus our lenses and seek out the positive spins in our tales. We learned that often- it's in how you tell it; that brings a story true to life, and rather than seeing ourselves as mere victims of our fate, we might instead start to see ourselves as warriors within our own battle stories.

For some, the process was indeed healing and cathartic. For others, it seemed as if it was anchoring; but mostly, there was a mutual feeling of validation and pride. We realised that no matter who you are and where you come from, or what your life story, every life story, like every person, always had worth.

Unfortunately, some individuals would remain a mystery; trapped inside their minds and bodies, with their stories never told, shared, or celebrated, and for me, this felt saddest and most tragic of all to have lived a life to a ripe age and not have a tale to tell- good, bad, or imaginary- felt like the most heart-breaking aspect of old age, disability, and chronic illness. Even though paradoxically speaking, it might also be argued- that for some, this might, in fact, be a blessing in disguise!

Mum knitting dad a jumper- to cope with the shock of the cold British Weather!

PREFACE

As a teen, I'd often esconder to my room, attempting to escape our frequently tumultuous household. While listening to 80's Madonna tracks, I'd fill in personal diaries, write poetry, stories, and songs, and sooner or later, someone would be heard hollering up the stairs after me-

"Mumooo! What are you doing up there- so long?"

"Writing my book!" I'd shout back.

- As if writing a book- was a perfectly normal preoccupation for a twelve-year-old girl! Most of my family would typically scoff and roll their eyes at me when I said such things, but my mum would be the only one to take my ambitions seriously and the only one who truly believed in my dreams. Even though, sadly, I rarely granted her the same faith; when she'd vainly suggest that-

"...if you want to write a good story- write mine!"

And I'd always laugh and dismiss her- "Yeah, alright, mum! Whatever!"

I can partly be excused for this naive oversight, as I wasn't fully versed in my mum's story. Besides, like most teenagers, I wasn't ready to accept that my mum was even interesting and cool enough for me to write about. Yet years on, I realise I seriously underestimated her and her story and kick myself- for not taking the time out sooner from all my selfish pursuits and for not giving her the time of day- to listen to her story. Now I realise that had I done this- I'd have gained an invaluable insight into her and her life. Her story was ready-made, with all the hooks and trappings synonymous with a blockbuster hit! From tragedy to triumph, secrets to scandals, love to heartache, dreamy adventures to disastrous despair! Besides the fact that her life story (although uncredited to her!) informed and inspired an actual Bollywood movie made in 1963, called- 'Tere Ghar Ke Samne' (*Opposite your house*), starring the 60's heartthrob- Dev Anand and the on-screen beauty of the day Nutan- maybe too, it wouldn't have taken me so long to appreciate that the most significant inspiration; was not to be found outside those alluring windows- from which I so often gazed; but was sat right beside me all along!

"A heart is not judged by how much you love; but by how much you are loved by others" L. Frank Baum
'The Wonderful Wizard Of Oz

My mums like a living angel; who has always supported me unconditionally. She's impeded my progress and proven to be that one shoulder to cry on, as well as that most trusted crash mat. She's my one person to count on- come what may! The more I know her, the more I want to know her and the more thankful I feel- for knowing her. Within this unique opportunity, while we gaze into her past, I'm blessed to get to know her as no one else has. This impetus to spend more quality time with her in our mature and wiser years has enabled me to rediscover her again.

It's my privilege and honour to help translate her story into this book. To help her fill in the blanks, using my creative imagination and writer's instinct, and enable her to leave a legacy, not only through her children and grandchildren- but through her own sacred story. This, in itself, is a gift- from her to me. From me to her. And from us to you.

INCEPTION

Although I realise that time travel isn't possible in the literal sense, I'm enthused to travel back in time via her memories. Journeying into her past, as if aboard a time travelling vessel, inside our mind's eye, we hope to inspire others to do the same. To travel back in time with their loved ones and find value and meaning; in listening to another person's tale. By catapulting ourselves into the vortex of the past, may we all be so lucky as to realise that even the most mundane people, even the most seemingly inconsequential lives, can sometimes surprise us. Once you take a closer look, you too might find someone's story unexpectedly enlightening, surprisingly inspiring, and profoundly moving, all the same.

Stop, Start, Finish!

> *"Life can only be understood by looking backwards; but it must be lived looking forward"* (Soren Kierkegaard, 1813-1855)

Sunday, 5th December 2010 @ 11 am- marks the start of our quest. Heavily pregnant with my first and only child- due next

Valentine's Day; my mum is keen to remind me of her prophesied prediction-

"You will see!" she reiterates; "...baby will come exact- my Birthday! I saw in my dream! 22nd January! Dekhi...! Tho dekhi! *(See...! You'll see!)*."

With a child in my womb and my mother by my side- recalling her childhood; there's a strange serendipity in the air. After pestering my husband for weeks, Christmas is finally up, and the festive ambience, warm blankets, soft cushions, and hot cardamon tea; have created the perfect cosy and cocooned atmosphere within which our nostalgia can float. We are both nervous and excited and share a familiar juvenile giggle; as we prepare for our trip down memory lane.

At first, keen on establishing all the bare facts, timelines, and a chronology of events, we are strangely formal and act as if conducting an official interview. But we share a common goal- to establish a solid foundation upon which to build our worded sculpture. As she speaks, some of her stories sound familiar, and others sound almost alien. Yet even within this specific retelling of the past- although contrived in purpose; it feels intrinsically unique between us. Like close friends, sharing deep secrets.

To start with, she's a little guarded and hesitant. Even somewhat confused as she recalls, over seventy years of her life, from the archives, of her mind! Google- has become my new best friend- for accuracy, historical referencing, contextualisation, and the correct translations of many Hindi words and phrases. She treads cautiously, trying to find steady ground beneath her feet. I try my best to remain patient and calm, to be a good daughter, listener, and friend. Now that I'm wise enough to know that although at times her story is eagerly forthcoming; with self-advocacy and almost a sense of urgency; at other times, it requires coaxing out of her with delicate, encouraging hands and also a soft voice of reason. I'm mindful of respecting her pain, as her trauma is delicate and fragile, much like she, and I sense her heart is still a little fractured. With the added language barrier, cultural differences, and differing perspectives- ascertaining a truthful context and a mutual viewpoint is more complex than I'd anticipated. Though we are the same blood relations, bonded in our ethereal connection, we are still intrinsically different. Our divergent backgrounds and life experiences skew our views apart on many pivotal things like religion, tradition, and philosophies of life. We see life through the prism of our selective vision boards.

Alongside copious amounts of tea, I write scatterings of words on paper and capture her ramblings inside my new Wizard of Oz notebook. After each session, I revisit my notes and, often, inconsistent scribbles in the witching hours of the night when I'm plagued with insomnia! I try to weave the notes into a story and collate them, word by word, sentence by sentence, moment by moment, thread by thread, until a vast tapestry of her life takes form.

In due course, I'll use my writer's instinct to find my central character's voice and establish my story's arc. I'll need to decide which points in time; to delve deeper into and which points; to scurry past. At times, her answers seem too simplistic, too, matter of fact and lack crucial, elaborative details—those necessary nuances to tell a good tale and things; that are essential in engaging or even seducing the listener and audience. Sometimes, she loses herself inside her memory, and I must steer her back to me. Other times, I push her further into her mind's eye; as if trying to extrapolate the pixie dust gathered upon the farthest-reaching shelves. At times, it is me; who's to blame for my indulgence, caught on the saddle of a racing horse and verbosely eager to create a clear picture—with my gaze, wanting to imbue my vision vicariously.

Mindful of her age, health, and capacity to cope- as too, my own! - I pace our chats and avoid either of us overdoing things and becoming physically and mentally overwhelmed. We share health-related limitations which affect our daily functions. We both suffer from daily pain and fatigue, and even our ability to give ourselves into a deep conversation itself; can sometimes prove too much.

At times, I'm ruthless, cherry-picking my way through a pick and mix of her memories as if deciding which sweets- I'd like to unwrap. Which sweets are too sweet, sour, or might otherwise lead to a comatose sugar rush and crash? Although she's the captain of our ship, I must be her trusted navigator to ensure we keep on track and ride all the waves between authenticity and imagination. Even when the waves crash, collide, and fold over each other; I must maintain that faint line between the captain and the sailor; the story and the storyteller; the truth and the fiction. At times, these lines inevitably blur amid a storm of ideas or while caught adrift.

Soon I forget that I am her daughter, and she is my mother. Soon, we become something more cerebral. Our connection and understanding transcend our mortal relation and take us into a new realm of synergy as if orbiting a new multiverse; one being to the other, one traveller to the next, one storyteller to another. Soon I realise that nothing is truly lost, or left behind, if only... it is remembered.

Clutching her now-cold mug of tea inside her wrinkled wary hands, she speaks of a little, whippersnapper girl she once knew—a girl at the precipice of youth and on the verge of a wanderlust journey. Like a new star, she is sparking into existence out of a black galaxy sky, and the embers in her eyes are as if igniting a whole new universe.

To mummy dearest, this book is a present from the past, with love x.

> *"The violets in the mountains have broken the rocks,"* Tennesse Williams.

Mum the bird whisperer with our beautiful rescue budgie Lakshmi

ACKNOWLEDGEMENT

It's taken too long to get here! Years of stopping and starting- due to health restrictions, distractions, and setbacks. Alongside life's many obligations, like many of us, all too often, feeling like we're spreading ourselves too thinly- as mothers, wives, daughters, sisters, and friends. It's taken having to sacrifice so much family time and so many socials with friends, (not easy for a people pleaser!) and almost becoming estranged from them; while I went down this rabbit hole of creative writing, from which even the slightest distraction; felt like a setback on my focus. It's taken overcoming many moments of self-doubt, lost courage, and a lack of motivation. It's taken carefully navigating a process of writing- which can work around so many daily debilitating symptoms, alongside days, weeks, and even months of flare-ups, which have continually impeded my progress. Aside from the endless doctors and hospital appointments and surgeries along the way, it's also taken many life-changing events and some catastrophes to finally get here!

- 2011- marked a traumatically long- 72-hour labour, leading to post-natal and post-traumatic stress, a flare-up of my illness, and the struggles of being a new mother-compounded by my debilitating condition.

- 2018- marked the sudden onset of life-threatening Sepsis. In a coma and on life support, after multiple organ failure, a laparoscopy, and total body paralysis, it was believed I had only hours left to live...! A miracle later, followed by three weeks in I.C.U., three months in rehab, and twelve months of gruelling convalescence- I was finally led back to my former baseline of health.

- 2019- marked my beloved husband suffering a major heart attack! (not even 40 yet!) Another miracle, followed by three stents and another lengthy recovery, negotiated against caring for our young son and me- he, too, defied many odds!

- 2020- marked a drastic decline in my father's health-needing full-time care and support and the prospect of *writing a book*,- a leisurely pursuit I could no longer justify or indulge!

- 2021- marked Dad's passing during Covid, following a traumatic hospital stay and limited visitation. Together with the unexpected deaths of two other close friends- a year apart and countless other friends and relatives; who seemed to be dropping dead like flies!

- 2022- marked a turning point. Coming out of gut-wrenching grief, depression, and health flare-ups, to rekindle some motivation and willpower to re-focus and resume my writing efforts. With that ever-distant finishing line alluding me; from maddening rewrites, creative redirections, technical setbacks, proofreads, and edits, before ready to finally self-publish! And the only constant;

that inner voice, however faint at times, insisting- *Never to give up!* Indeed, writing this book (Although, a labour of love and at times, fun, exciting, and even cathartic!) has also proven to be the hardest thing I've ever done! Whosoever thinks (looking in from the outside) it's an easy feat...well, I dare you to have a go and you, too, might find- it was all worth it- *in the end!*

Me and mum eating chaat at our local Indian

DEDICATIONS

For Mummy dearest- the epitome of maternal love personified, the true matriarch of our family, and my greatest muse. Thank you for surviving, trusting me with your story, sharing it with courage, resolve, and free abandon, and for being my Mum. You inspire me every day. I'm so proud of you and absolutely love you!

For Ian- my symbiotic supporter. The very wind beneath my wings. Thank you for heating my endlessly cold mugs of tea and coffee and giving the best massages! For keeping house and home- like a single parent, at times! You've proven my most significant pillar of strength, my most constructive critic, my most robust and reliable push-up bar, my trusted shoulder to cry on, my emotional crutch, and my Mr. Motivator- when I needed it most. Thank you for not giving up on me or my dreams and for unconditionally embracing and accepting my authenticity. Your encouragement, love, and support have been invaluable, without which, I'd never have realised this dream. Love you truly, madly, deeply.

For Dad- I wish you were here to witness this achievement and finally say- '...you are proud!' The fire in my belly comes from you and your doubts and disapprovals, which often fueled my rebel heart! I wish I'd known you better, appreciated you more, and given you more time, patience, and love without irreverence. Wish I'd held onto more of yours, also. You proved a better Grandad than Dad and I, retrospectively- a better mother; than daughter. But now I know why? You, too, carried your wounds- unhealed, unpacked, unspoken, which shaped you; for better or worse. I've finally accepted you for you and in spite of you. I miss you and all your idiosyncrasies. Even your grumpy, frowning face! Mostly, I miss your infectious, unapologetic laughter while watching Johnny Lever, Benny Hill, Laurel & Hardy, and Only Fools & Horses and hearing you holler- "Kamaal hai!" *(It's amazing!)*

For Aramis- my most incredible legacy. Hope you'll be inspired; seeing Mum committed to her goals, working so hard to achieve them- even against all the odds! Hope you, too, walk your path with courage and conviction and push hard for your dreams. Lujew, long time!

For Bebs- my kindred-spirited confidante/fierce-warrior friend/onstage mum/offstage Angel. I desperately miss you. You taught me how to stop and smell the roses, search for rainbows, find silver linings, hug trees, be creative & crafty, dance- like no one is watching, laugh- like it were medicine for your soul! Your childlike eccentricity, positivity, humour, innate wisdom, zest, and colour- were always infectious and inspiring. You were magic! And even now, your pixie dust remains as if sprinkled inside my fondest memories of you. Our time spent could never have proved enough! I adore you!

For Gizmo (my ragdoll cat!)- So wonderfully purrrfect Your cocooned being of calm and fluffiest cuddles- often plug me back to life and remind me of life's simplest pleasures, like watching you catch flies, roll in the sun, and lick snowflakes off the grass. Stroking your soft fur and gazing into your galaxy-blue eyes- I'm always reminded that Life & Cats are precious gifts. Gijew-love-forever!

For migrants searching for better lives abroad, with suitcases full of dreams. For those that brazenly pave their way through intolerance, ignorance, hate, and injustice and claw out from beneath victimisation and terror- determined to survive and thrive. For those who break through those glass ceilings built to limit growth and stifle progress. You are the very bedrock and pinnacle of this rich tapestry, which makes up this robust, modern, multicultural Britain- we all call home, and for that, I salute you!

For mothers, daughters, and granddaughters. For fathers, sons, grandsons, and all caregivers- who nurture our fruits of tomorrow. For those who've loved and lost. For those who feel lost and wounded by traumatic childhood experiences or ravaged by their pasts. For those surviving domestic abuse, neglect, violence, sexual molestation, and addiction. For those carrying grief and its insurmountable burden of pain or regret. For families holding dark secrets- like weighted luggage on their souls. For children who've been hurt and unintentionally become adults- who hurt. Hurt people hurt...unless they heal. For those struggling with mental health issues or battling the shame, stigma, ignorance, and silence that comes with it. For those whose dreams burn like embers of desires- keep listening to your inner voice- "Never give up!" For those who fight for their dreams and aspirations- against all the odds, against illness, disability, and ostracisation. May we reach our dreams and inspire others to do the same. Ultimately, our dreams are often just a set of goals- yet to be realised. I dedicate this story to all of you.

The stories of our parents, aunties, uncles, grandparents, and ancestors hold our most significant pool of wealth and the keys which unlock our humanity and sense of community. I hope to inspire you to sit beside one another while you still can. Listen to their story while you still can. Take stock, take notes, record, and document- while you still can. One day, these stories from our pasts; these stories of all those we've met, loved, and lost- shall be all that remains to honour them and even, to honour you. It is inside a flickering memory, upon the lips of a storyteller, or in ink written on paper where our lives and stories live on and might dance like fireflies- alight at night, so long after the darkness has swallowed us all. Our stories are precious. They deserve to be told, heard, shared, and remembered. For beyond our procured earthly pleasures and treasures and our unquenchable thirst for materials, our stories hold the most value. They are the most fundamental and meaningful part of our existence. A looking glass to search our souls and a compass to trace us back on our journey. From one person to another. One generation to the next. One soul to another. We must seek out the stories, especially from the elders in our families and our communities; before it's too late, their words are left unspoken, and their tales are left untold, forever buried with them inside their lonely graves. Collect these stories fervently, like lucky pennies, spent into our legacies. Pay homage to them, our ancestral roots, and the trees of our nature.

With every branch, every leaf, and every tiny little sapling or blossoming flower- they all form part of the whole. They are connected. We are connected. No matter how twisted, torn, rotten, mangled, naked, or bare- we must collect them- unedited, exposing- the good, the bad, and the ugly- warts and all. Dig deeper with your inner child's curiosity and confront your demons.

Know every inch of its face- like the back of your hand. We must embrace our scars- like ink marks on our souls. Acknowledging the past; is to carve out a more transparent future. Knowing what's been; helps us know- what's to come and also know ourselves deeper now.

We are each a star in our little show. We are the protagonists in our tales and the echoes of lost songs. We are the horse whisperers of our stud and carriers of the baton and connect our tribe in the truest sense. To conquer our pasts, we must embrace our lost tales before we can truly rise as phoenixes, out of those ashes and into our future. Before, we can feel unencumbered by our courage to speak our truth. Even when the truth hurts, may it also set us free. And after the hurt... it is time to heal.

"Pain is inevitable, but suffering is optional"
Haruki Murakami

PROLOGUE

"For time is the longest distance between two places" Tennesse Williams

MOURNING

"HE'S DEAD!" Mum sighed, placing the phone receiver down and barely noticing me as I entered the room.

"Huh... who's dead?" I yawned, flopping onto the sofa next to my dad- in disbelief- he was already on his mid-morning nap when I'd just woken up!

"Dad's dead..." She said, cool as a cucumber.

"What!?"

"I said- he is dead!" She looked vaguely into space.

"Dad's dead!? Oh my God! Dad! Dad?" Suddenly, I'd clocked my dad- slumped over in his armchair and not a single snore or grunt- coming out!

"No! Shush! Idiot! Not your dad- pagal! *(Stupid!)* ... my dad! Your Nanaji! Your dad is just sleeping!" she sighed, shaking her head at me.

"Oh! What the f'...mum! You scared me to death- en'all!"

I took in a huge sigh of relief, having stopped myself from manhandling Dad- just in time! He- none the wiser, suddenly let out an almighty snort and resumed his expected, wall-thundering snores! Alas... he was alive! (The only time- the sound of his snores, was a welcomed relief!) I tried to register and calm myself as I watched Mum walk towards the hallway mirror and stop to fix her hair and face. Just as the phone rang and startled our hearts and I ran to answer it.

"Hello?"

"Hello sweetheart. Is our Sue there? Just want to check she's coming to work today for overtime?" the nice lady asked. It always sounded sweet, when they called mum- *Sue*.

"Oh... Umm... I don't think so, you see, her dad has just..."

Suddenly, mum snatched the phone off me.

"Hello? Yes, it's Sue, I am coming now. See you in one hour, Mrs Smith. Ok, Bye-Bye!"

Mum put the phone down and returned to fix herself in the mirror. Suddenly I had so many questions- alongside some which I thought best to leave inside my head! Like- ...Why are you acting so bloody calm and not crying- if your dads just died? And still getting ready for overtime at work- as if it's just another ordinary Saturday morning!?

"Mum are you sure you are alright to go work?"

"Yes. I'm fine. Good... it's good he is finally dead! Shame... he didn't die sooner!" She suddenly blurted, before opening the front door and walking straight through it. Though stunned in disbelief, I said nothing, not even Goodbye!

EVENING

That evening, Mum had put on another one of her boring, three-and-a-half-hour-long, old black & white Bollywood Movies (before my love affair with old movies, began!) As usual, Dad was quickly off to the land of nod, seconds after claiming- 'he wasn't sleepy, but merely resting his eyes for a minute!' as we decided to make a run for it and go play outside with the neighbours, in the formerly safe local streets! After almost four hours had passed and all the Neighbours' kids had been summoned in for dinner; with no sign of mum; yelling from our doorstep- we rushed back home, to find Mum, still sat in the very same spot, we'd left her in and still watching the rolling credits of her ridiculously long movie! Though now, she was in floods of tears, whilst transfixed to the screen. Dad, just as we'd left him, was snoring loud enough to rattle the coffee table beside him! Unsure whether Mum's tears were brought on by the movie's expected dramatic and emotional climax (which always made her ball!) or else, finally, a sign of her grief; we paid little attention, as my brother and sister, ran towards the bubbling pot on the stove and were instantly caught in a jostle for the giant ladle- both wanting to be first to pour their aloo *(Potatoe)* curry and rice, into their bowls. As usual, oblivious to sharing, they'd already served up most of the pot's contents! Deciding to wait my turn and unwilling to get caught in the crossfire, I turned to mum.

"Mum, it's not real! It's just a movie! Why you getting so upset?" I tried to reason with her as I slammed my sweaty head onto the crochet mat, covering the sofa's top edge.

"It is real!" She surprisingly replied, sniveling into her chunni scarf and straightening the crochet mat, under my head.

As we sat to eat, Mum hastily prepared fresh chapatis for Dad. Clocking the VCR movie cover, I noticed the face of the hunky Bollywood hero- 'Dev Anand'- who shared not only our surname but also the drooling admiration of most of my horny aunties!

"Mum? What does te... tere... gha... gaaar ki samon... samonay- mean?" I asked, struggling to pronounce the Hindi title correctly. "Tere Ghar Ke Samne!" she snapped- correcting me, "It means- *House opposite* and believe it or not...

THIS IS MY STORY...

1

FRACTURED

"You forget what you want to remember and remember what you want to forget" Cormac McCarthy

RIPPED

Sat perched on the edge of her bed, she carefully stitched her salwar trouser, which had, yet again, mysteriously ripped and frayed at the very same section of her hemline- between her legs. Squinting her eyes, she struggled to see the end of the white thread; she'd been trying to feed into the eye of the needle for quite some time. She wondered *if she, too, might soon need spectacles- like her brother Raj?* Though most likely, it was just the sheer lack of sleep which was the actual cause of her blurred vision. Nonetheless, simply imagining her father's reaction- for the added expense on their already strained finances; was enough to strike fear into her heart and put her stomach into spasms. Alongside this was the sudden realisation- that daylight was quickly becoming scarce and soon...it would be *dark!*

At night, when it was dark; when she was illusively caught between her forming dreams and the soft pillow beneath her cheeks; she'd always experience strange, deep anxiety and apprehension. Feeling almost paralysed, while held hostage inside a peculiar haze of uncertainty, she'd hear distant echoing whispers, calling her in and out of her slumber. Barely able to breathe, she'd quietly beg for the light of day to come quickly and save her. To offer its tiny droplets of hope and escape within its embers of morning dew. It was almost always in her sleep when she'd feel those strangest sensations. Like being inside and outside herself at once and taken someplace else while still being present. When a dark, all-consuming abyss surrounded her like a foul-breathing hungry beast.

Thread, finally in, she hurried to finish sewing her seam, desperate to complete the last few stitches before it was too late. In her haste, she accidentally pricked her finger. Sucking in the air sharply, she noticed a tiny blob of blood on the tip of her finger and felt a strange urge to squeeze out more as if it was calling for release.

Just then, her mother's anticipated evening call came blaring through the corridor- requesting her prompt help in the kitchen.

BEAUTY

Covered head to toe in her elder sister's hand-me-down rejects, her meek body appeared as if shrouded beneath a giant potato sack- plonked on as if to shield her chastity and hide any forming figure. Her salwar trousers- loose and baggy; resembled the attire of a poor street clown- with ridiculously long and wide ankle hems rolled halfway up her legs. Like a little beggar child; caught adrift from a storm, she often marooned the house and large courtyard; quietly in the shadows, like a ghost. Yet still, her innate beauty was impossible to deny. Even at the tender age of eight and while dressed in the most unflattering of clothes, without any care and concern- it seemed that her delicate undeclared prettiness still peered gently from beneath everything she wore. Like an emerging peacock waiting for its chance to proudly display nature's artistry through the glorious eruption of its feathered train, she, too, held fast to that quiet promise inside her shy and graceful poise. Her fair and bright face, perfectly framed like a portrait of art, between the shadows of her onyx locks- which, even when messily twisted out of the way to the top of her head, still appeared so effortlessly beautiful; made her a rare breed. One of those select few, most envied of girls- whose radiance and serenity shone through any cover-up. Even when unannounced, even without trying and even without deliberation and intention; it innocently evoked many voyeuristic stares and the bulging, beady eyes; which fixated upon her form, chased her little footsteps, and searched her out from the shadows, everywhere she went, even without her knowing.

POOR-KING'S DINNER

After hours of exhausting preparation; confined within her stiflingly hot kitchen; her mother; now tired- to her brittle bones, sighed with relief! Finally, she had finished cooking the extravagant feast she'd been slaving over since dawn! It was not a feast for any prestigious visitor or V.I.P dignitary, or even for a regular visit from family or friends- No, it was merely a feast to appease her ever-fussy, ever-demanding, ever hungry- husband! He- a self-declared reigning king within their home, afforded her little notice, let alone any appreciation, for the significant effort required to prepare such a lavish dinner on a regular Friday night!

5 am sharp; he'd reeled off the extensive list of his choice preferences as if instructing his personal sue chef! Whether the ingredients required were available or not, expensive or not, even in season, was of little consequence to him. He wanted what he wanted when he wanted it- period! And any deviation from his wants was always presumed to demonstrate insolence if not work-shy, laziness!

PENCHANT

Her mother carefully plated each item onto their father's personal silver tray. His dishes and special silver tray; were forbidden to use by any other. His food was always made fresh and kept separate from the rest; for in his grandiose opinion- 'It would otherwise make everything- ort!' She meticulously lined up the steaming hot bowls and carefully reeled off her mental menu checklist to ensure- nothing was missed!

Starters- spicy, roasted poppadom's. Main- Paneer curry *(curdled cheese curry)*, freshly prepared Saag *(spinach curry)*, and Urid Daal *(brown, lentil curry)* with perfectly fluffy- Pilau Rice and perfectly round, thin, and inflated fresh Chapattis. Sides- Homemade Cucumber Raita *(seasoned yoghurt)*, Homemade spicy pickles, and Indian salad with fresh whole green chillies. Dessert- Sweet Milk Semiya *(Vermicelli noodles cooked in sweet cardamon-flavoured milk)*; everything needed to be cooked and presented precisely how he liked it. A Master Chef at work in her kitchen, she'd use expert precision to diligently create her perfect signature dishes for him, always against the clock- like a ticking time bomb in her midst. Garnishing each bowl with either freshly cut coriander leaves, slithers of fresh ginger, or chopped fresh green chillis- she finally sprinkled the pretty crisscross pattern flourish of masala powder over his yoghurt (just how he liked it!) before grabbing a kitchen towel and carefully wiping away any excess mess, from the edges of the bowls. He was a stickler for details, and like a sergeant major at an army base; he would inspect every inch of his troops and their belongings. He would notice any tiny little mistake, any slight change or inconsistency- which would otherwise deviate from the expected taste, appearance, even scent- of all things. In an instance- too much or too little of anything, even salt, could annoy him. Too much or too little chilli could frustrate him, and the slightest discrepancy and oversight; could quickly send him into a gloriously foul mood, if not a fit of fury! Even a slightly messy bowl itself; could prove enough for his deep contention; within this most delicately balanced and tumultuous of households!

"Khaaanaaa! *(Foooood!)*" His voice roared through the corridor. His now-second call for dinner!

Her mother nervously handed Sudesh the tray before instructing, "Acha laija achi larkhi jaldi upne Papaji kai liye! *(Ok, take this good girl, quickly for your father!)*."

Cautiously taking hold of the heavy tray and just about to turn and leave, her mother suddenly grabbed her arm again-

"Thahar ja! Doh chucker ker ke lai ja! Bhagwan nahin kare, sub gir na jiye! *(Wait! Do two rounds and take it! God-forbid, it all falls!)*." She warned.

Rolling her eyes at her mother, she instead pulled away, feeling too impatient to carry out two journeys- back and forth from the kitchen. Ignoring her mother's wishes, she swiftly proceeded, eager to return to sewing as quickly as possible and, most importantly- before it was *dark!* She knew her mother would not allow her to continue sewing after dark. The household rules- regarding activities after dark had always been crystal clear! There was to be No sewing- after dark! No sweeping- after dark! No cutting of fingernails- after dark! No touching or watering plants- after dark! No D.I.Y jobs- after dark! And no shaking of keys- after dark!

Along with most of the other elders in the community, her mother was a staunchly religious and superstitious person; who strongly believed it was bad luck to carry out specific tasks- after dark! For years, the children had been told, story after story, of instances when people had ignored these crucial- karmic rules- said to have been passed down by their ancestors and, in turn, paid a hefty price for their penance! It was noted that each person, on each occasion, had retrospectively experienced some form of bad luck, misfortune, or curse, which was believed to be attributed to their unforgivable disobedience and disregard of these strict rules. Person after person, who'd become the victim of these seemingly ruthless, vengeful, and cynical Gods- intent to punish nihilist thinkers and reassert their sadistic power and control; over the helpless and forsaken lives of their disciples. The timely coincidences of all the dire occurrences- proved to be more than enough for all to be fully convinced; of this karmic reckoning and enough to strike fear into their wanton hearts!

SERVICE!

"Fear is a potion that poisons our strength" Aramis
Noah Shad

Tightly gripping the sharp edges of the tray, almost half the size of her body; she stomped forward as the steaming bowls sat like bubbling baby volcanoes beneath her chin. Releasing their spicy vapours into her nostrils and making her nose unwittingly twitch, her body wobbled, trying to keep balance beneath the tray, as her vision was also obscured from the rising mists. Each perilous step toward her father gave her a strange fluttering feeling inside her belly. Just then, she heard his- third call for dinner, followed by her mother's voice hollering from the kitchen.

"Oh-ho! Sudesh...di bachchi! Suna nahin? *(...Child!! Didn't you hear?)*"

Shaking her head in dismay, her mother could only pray to herself that- *her husband's dinner would reach him without any problems!* Then, suddenly noticing the daylight's descent, she, too, hurriedly started to sweep her kitchen floors; also conscious of the fact that soon...it would be dark!

"Khaana milega!- ya nahin? *(Will I get food- or not?)*." Her father bellowed out with his now-fourth call for dinner!

His impatient voice reverberated so loud- that it caused Sudesh to flinch unwittingly; while stumbling forward and trying her best to keep a grip on her heavy tray. Having almost reached the end of the corridor, her heart raced, as her clammy fingers, struggled to keep their hold. Suddenly, she noticed some of the contents of the bowls had accidentally spilled over the edges. Gasping aloud as a sudden bolt of terror ran through her body, she knew her father would be little than impressed; when she'd arrive with his dinner- not just late, but also presented in a messy tray! Hastily tilting the tray back in the opposite direction, she tried to avoid more spillage. But instead, she'd inadvertently overcompensated and spilled even more of the food! Caught in utter panic and having lost both her senses and her last remaining grip, her legs finally gave way beneath her, and she went tumbling onto the floor in an almighty...

Craaaaaaaaaaaaaash!!! Everything spilled everywhere!

The almost deafening cacophony from the silver tray, bowls, and utensils- all falling onto the concrete floors, alongside the sound of her thudding body; had shaken the entire house. The bowls and utensils; continued to clink, clank, clonk, and ricochet their way, across the wall and floors, as her father's entire feast; covered her body and clothes and instantly tainted them in the brown and yellow, turmeric-laden liquids. A sight of utter devastation; the yucky steaming sludge of food, now having decorated the entire corridor and even the ceiling, looked more like the aftermath of a dog's diarrhetic poo mixed with someone's sudden projectile vomit! Food particles were now dripping and trickling from everywhere, even above her head, as she sat on the floor, stunned in shock and utter disbelief! Suddenly, she felt a stinging and burning sensation coming from her deeply grazed knees, where she'd hit the floor hardest and scolded her naked skin; with the piping hot food! Hissing like an injured alley-cat, she apprehensively looked up to find her mother, now standing in front of her, with her face in her trembling hands and an expression of pure terror traced across it! For a moment; too consumed by the horror of it all, they both locked eyes; unsure of what to do next. Within a split second, her mother's hands had already pre-

STITCHED UP SUE!

empted her daughter's oncoming screams, as she lunged forward, and instinctively covered Sudesh's open mouth, only muffling the sound. Then, as if in a sudden frenzy, her mother leaped forward, harshly grabbed Sudesh from the pit of her arms, and pulled her up; as a fleetingly naive thought entered her confused head...

Maybe, she could still somehow salvage the situation? Before he got heed of it and turned up!?

But before she'd even managed to get Sudesh off the floor, they were both stopped dead in their tracks; after hearing the familiar sound of approaching footsteps! Then, with their hearts skipping a beat and their breaths caught inside their constricted throats, they both looked at one another with the same pitiful expression of terror, having realised the same thing at the same time...

It's too late! He's coming!

After a momentary silent stand-off- where no one was quite sure what to say or do next; the roaring sound of his voice abruptly broke the silence, instantly firing profanities at them like deadly bullets filled with venom! Sudesh slowly started to crawl back, dragging the sludge of wasted food under her soggy bottom and sliding across the concrete floor like a slithering snake in retreat. But she knew it wouldn't be long before her father's rage transpired from his sharp-cutting tongue into his hands, fists, and feet! At which point, all hell would break loose! Suddenly and rather intuitively, her mother had sprung forward, just in time to intercept the heavy-handed thrust of her husband's slap right before it reached her daughter's face! But, instead, it struck her mother! Sending her hurtling down the corridor, landing smack-bang on the kitchen door's sharp metal handle, and instantly cutting her head open! Sudesh watched on from behind her father.

She could only make out her mother's figure, now crouched in a foetus position, as she cried out in intense pain. Too scared to move a muscle, even though desperately wanting to go to her mother's side, she remained frozen as her bladder gave way and her urine soaked through to her salwar pants. Knowing what would come next, she watched as her father pushed further toward her mother. Still undeterred, still unsatisfied, and ready to strike down again. He continued to shout profanities as he released his rage; shoving, kicking, slapping, and punching her mother as if the devil himself had him by his limbs and had deafened his ears- to her cries for mercy. Her screams, soon rhythmically following each assault to her flesh, as Sudesh simply watched on, looking half dazed, half transfixed, and all the time knowing; that there was nothing that she could do to stop him. He was beyond all reproach, beyond any mercy, and unstoppable. As usual, all she could do was quietly pray *that at some point soon, he'd tire... before her mother took her very last breath!*

Soon, even her mother's cries had succumbed to a slight whimper, like an animal who'd been tirelessly hunted down and brutally ravaged by a predator. Now, it simply lay there. Too exhausted to fight back. Too far gone, defeated to run away and entirely surrendered to its impending doom while quietly waiting for the sweetest salvation of death itself! After a while, it looked as if her father were merely pounding his fists upon a lifeless stuffed puppet or an old sack of potatoes- disregarded upon the floor. Then, sensing a presence, Sudesh slowly turned her head in the opposite direction, and through the haze of her blurry tears, she could only just make out the faintest outlines of her sibling's small figures. All lined up at the end of the hallway like ghostly shadows. All silently stood and watching on, like muzzled and paralysed dogs- commanded to 'Stay!' and simply observing his enviable spirit, dancing within its rampant rage.

After a while, all that remained were the intermittent sounds of their breaths. Some- slow, staggered, laboured, and restricted, and others forcefully loud and filled with adrenaline and defiance- just like his! Each inhaled and exhaled that limited oxygen supply in the air, from in and out of their still-forming lungs.

Then, as if she was moving without any real intention or effort, she found her hands were slowly picking up the mess surrounding her. Her body wasn't hers anymore, and her hands were moving; on their own accord as if responding to an innate need to be proactive and do something- anything, which could somehow make some sense. Even if it was; simply cleaning up! Continually scooping the remnants of the still-warm food into her trembling palms and pouring it back into the scattered steel bowls, she sat as if collecting muddy ashes, left on a funeral pyre after someone's death, followed by the floods of a tropical monsoon.

She wished she could disappear before her father's gaze landed on her again. She begged God; *he'd at least be appeased- by her clear signs of subservience, obedience, and compliance*, and she wanted to say- 'Look, papaji, Look! I'm such a good girl!' But he wasn't done yet! Now, with his attention back on her again, he turned towards her as a sudden bolt of terror rushed through every cell of her body and pricked up every tiny hair upon her skin. Unsure whether she should stay still, carry on cleaning, or run for her dear life! - Her mind was ablaze with uncertainty and panic as a bombardment of conflicting messages started to scream inside her head-

"Run- Sudesh! No! Hide- Sudesh! No! Stop- Sudesh! No! Stay- Sudesh!... Bad! Bad! Bad! Sudesh!"

Instead, she slowly moved towards her mother, lying lifeless on the floor. With her back tightly braced against the cold stone of the corridor walls, she slid her body past her father's glare, wishing she could submerge into its very rock. But just as she reached her mother, she noticed her- as if coming back to life again and reawakening from a deep sleep. Suddenly, she was again startled; by her mother's unexpected onset of screeching cries! She looked at her mother, perplexed by the origins of her pain, especially given that her father was now far from her! The deep guttural sound coming from her mother was a sound she knew she would never forget. It was unlike anything she'd ever heard- almost inhuman and sliced like a knife inside her ears. She instantly knew; that something was terribly, terribly wrong! Her mother's hands were now clenched over her head as if trying to hold her brain inside her scalp before a red gush spewed between her clenched fingers, like a burst water pipe carrying a flood of red paint. Spitting and spewing the brightest RED- she'd ever seen!

INVISIBLE DOLL

> *"I know now that there is no one thing that is true- it is all true"* Earnest Hemingway

Their mother lay still and quiet on a white bed inside a drabby white room. People wearing white coats and gloves busied themselves, doing things around her, putting things into her, taking things out of her. Their busy, white-gloved hands moved as if they belonged to a magician, desperately trying to create some magic. Tubes poked into her arms like translucent snakes as smaller saplings seemed to be sucking her blood and feeding from her fountain of life—while other conduits carried nectar-like medicine into her veins like tunnels restocking her vast sea.

A small singular window was open to one side and provided an occasional and welcomed cool breeze. The stagnant sanitised air in the room, alongside the sickening foul smells; competed for space; hanging like invisible bubbles in the air from vapourised vomit, sweat, blood, medicines, and other harsh chlorinated chemicals. The dirty and dusty windowsills, covered in old cobwebs, gathered around the chipped edges of the paint-stripped wooden frames like a testimony of time passed. Pulling and pushing to and fro, the cobwebs barely clung on as their weak threaded fibres were gradually plucked away from their wanton grip. One by one, each was taken by the harsh, relentless winds. Some, much stronger than they appeared, still hung on; so unexpectedly tightly, even while half tethered and half ripped to shreds. Even while almost entirely lost to the harsh wind, they held on as if too frightened to let go.

A discoloured ripped floral curtain; billowed up and over the edges of the window frame, like wings, cascading and swaying back and forth, twisting in and out of itself, creating mini cyclones. Sudesh watched it- transfixed as her imagination wondered, and she conjured a floral dress draped over an invisible doll and the image of a spinning aged ballerina supremo- desperately holding onto her past glory days. With her tired, swollen feet; tightly squeezed inside her tattered red ballet shoes, she is a star upon her proscenium arch stage, caught inside a time warp of fame and lit up inside her illuminating spotlight. The rays of her sunlit past gleaming alongside the lines of white teethed smiles of adoration from the packed auditorium. Her eyes firmly shut, she continues to deny the day, to deny reality and refute the cruel race of time. Unaware that the show has ended, that the audience has long since left, and that the illusory applause she hears; is merely the sound of the pattering rain above her head- dripping from the fractured tiles of the formerly ornate and opulent, grand Elizabethan roof.

Sudesh could hear a bird chirping outside the window. Its persistent song as if calling for attention from the giant baron sky- seemingly deafened to its call. Occasionally, sharp beeping alarm sounds startled their little hearts and reignited that sense of urgency, alongside the hurried and hushed voices rushing past in the white corridors and in and out of the adjacent rooms. Faces, moist with droplets of sweat, like translucent water bubbles perched upon sand-dune skins, darted in and out of view. As she looked at her mother, she was mesmerised by the anticipated fall of the marble droplets upon her forehead, which clung to her green and blue, earth-tinted pastures of skin and sat inside the deep canyons cut across her swollen face. A white bandage, tightly wrapped around her mother's head, seemed to hold her skull in its correct place and stop the red paint from pouring out. A single reddish-pink blotch, peeping through from beneath the layers of muslin cloth like a giant marking of a bridal Bindi spot, coincidentally placed in the centre of her mother's forehead, was like the mark of the beast to whom she'd foolishly betrothed her atoned and forsaken life. That werewolf, wearing his illusory Gentleman's suit. That devil, dressed in grace, hiding his beastly demons beneath his porcelain skin. Her mother's expression was sullen and thoughtful. Her gaze, too, seemed transfixed towards the window. As if she, too, was watching the invisible ballet dancer dancing in her floral dress. Her neck was wrinkled from the tilt of her head, exaggerating the shiny, sweaty folds of her moist sunken skin. She was full of pain as she lay beneath those fresh white cotton sheets with her bloody-red, pink, green, blue, and yellow-marked body, like a destroyed rainbow in its wake. She was an entire dying world, lying on the bed. Her single plait of hair lay matted to one side, flattened with her sweat and grease, and limp like a dead centipede. She reeked of sweat, blood, urine, and faintly still of last night's uneaten dinner. The smell of stale curry, like a freshly killed carcass marinated in rotten old spices- made them all want to heave. She appeared older than just the night before, barely recognisable, and the strangeness in her face and the strangeness of this place terrified them all.

With her brothers and sisters lined up next to her, Sudesh nuzzled herself into a small space between them. She, too, wanted to keep a keen eye on her mother. For she, too, feared the very same thing- that if she looked away for too long... her mother might disappear!

POLICEMAN

"The only lies for which we are truly punished are those we tell ourselves" V.S. Naipaul

A tall, broad-shouldered policeman with a serious face sat at their mother's bedside. Using his ballpoint pen, he scribbled a few hurried notes on his notepad- placed upon his perfectly creased trouser leg. Freshly shaven, clean, and smart, his shiny slick black hair was perfectly set to one side of his head and matted down with what smelt like- mustard oil. The top surface of his hair glistened as it caught the single shard of sunlight and shimmered like a black whale's hump, peeping beneath the sea's surface. A single strand of his hair stood apart and erected right at the top of his head. Separated from the others, it swayed side to side like a blade of grass dancing in the breeze. Sudesh fought a sudden urge to reach over and ease it neatly back into its correct place. For such little things- always bothered her so! But she knew better than to touch a stranger, especially not one wearing a police uniform and with a serious expression on his face!

The Policeman, too, was sweating profusely. It sure was too hot a day; to wear a full police uniform and such heavy black leather boots! He reached to open his shirt's top button as sweat dripped off his forehead. Occasionally, he'd wipe his sweat away with a single sweep of his large dark hand. The floral curtain and the Policeman's single strand of hair seemed to be dancing in unison as if both were caught on the same timely breeze. Suddenly, the Policeman looked up and straight at Sudesh, catching her off guard, staring right at him! Quickly lowering her sight line, she soon realised; he wasn't looking at her, but more so, looking straight through her in deep thought. He sighed as he leaned closer to her mother and looked intently into her face as if trying to read something discreetly written upon her tightly pierced lips. Yet her mother's distant gaze remained fixed on the window, and she remained oblivious to his study of her face. Oblivious to her pleading children and oblivious too- to the whole world.

"Yes... then Mrs Sethji...aap, esure ho na? *(You are sure?)* Nuthing elze jew vill like it, to tell to mees? nuthing elze, jew is wanting to essay?"

Judging from his modern appearance, Sudesh was startled by his poor command of English. His thick Indian accent and high-pitched voice jarred with her expectation, especially given his foreboding form. They all waited for their mother to respond. It was a long, uncomfortable wait, and the silence was almost unbearable. But finally, she reacted...! Yet, with nothing more than the gentlest shake of her head. She had said nothing! Nothing at all!

"Jew nor... vee all is- aaaall here- is to help to jew... see jews is the having nor need be escared, Mrs Sethji," The Policeman persisted.

Finally, the Policeman became aware of his stray hair, and with one gentle sweep of his hand; he'd returned it to its rightful place.

"It is the bery eserious- this ematter, madamji. Jor skull, cud bin efractured! Yous cud bin death! It is not esmall ting. Jews ecould have bin ekilled...!" (He hesitated and stopped and looked at the line of children- with sympathy pouring from his eyes) "...meanings is- these this vons, elittle vones... aaaall these echilldrains, cub have ebin orphans- noh!? Who vill takes the care, huh...? Who... will take?"

Their mother slowly turned. She looked at her children, and for a split second, they all held their breaths, anticipating that slightest glimmer of hope hidden deep within her sullen eyes, momentarily lifting their spirits as they waited for her to speak. But after another fleeting moment, the hope was gone; when her gaze returned to the window, and her unshed tears sat stubbornly inside the wells of her eyes. Sudesh prayed desperately- *for her mother's tears to fall! For them to shed like giant waterfalls and release all the truth with them.* She wished; *the Policeman would notice them and would say something more- do something more- anything, but nothing at all!* But he didn't seem to notice, and he didn't say or do anything. He didn't even seem to care!

"Ac... ac... acci... accident...!" Their mother stuttered.

It was the one word; they'd least wanted to hear. And it was an utter lie. *A Big fat ugly lie!* Even though they'd always been told to tell the truth, how easy it seemed to tell a lie. And just like that; just like their father's giant sandaled foot; coming down and crushing their tiny ant-like beings- the truth, too, had been entirely stomped out. That flickering ember of fire, all but extinguished, into ashes. The Policeman sighed deeply-

"And jew...are jew... ehundred percent esure... esure- it vas the actually the ac... accident... Nor, nor bud-he push to jew? Esure? No push?"

It was like he knew! Like he knew *exactly* what had taken place, and yet, could not concede. Their mother nodded, and the Policeman, with his crestfallen face, sighed. He carried the echoes of their burdens in his sighs, and it seemed it was all he could do- sigh! He looked at the children, with his pitiful helplessness, making them all reel, before he sat up straight again as if having so readily admitted defeat! His annoying stray strand of hair; was separated from the rest and again, teasing in its dance. As her anger rose, Sudesh fought off the desire to slap his strand of hair onto his head! She wished someone would say something- anything! But even her eldest siblings; had lost all their fight. *Why is nobody speaking? Why is no one saying something more? Why doesn't anyone ever speak the truth?* Her helpless heart cried.

She felt like punching the Policeman in his smug face and screaming at him- until his ears could not hear anymore! He'd failed her! He'd failed them all! She felt like screaming at her mother, too! She felt like screaming at the whole world! The Policeman quietly took his leave, taking all the hope in the world with him as if contained inside the unused ink of his ballpoint pen. She hated her mother- for not telling the truth. She felt like ripping off her mother's bandages and letting the red paint- pour out and turn everything red forever! She wanted to scream- 'Look! Look! It was not an accident!' She felt like yanking the saplings and starving them of their mutual feed: their cursed, soul-destroying needs and desperate dependability upon this forsaken fountain of life.

The single ray of sunlight was gone. The ballerina supremo- had finally hung up her red shoes, accepting the show's bitter end. Even the chirping bird outside had stopped its call- now that each of them was stranded once again, stranded from the truth and stranded in the storm, all-knowing, so it shall perdure...

2

ELEUTHEROMANIA

"When things are difficult remember who you are"
Charle Mackesy

MONIKER

Her nickname at home had somehow become a tossup between- Naane, Naare, and Naanay. She had little idea where her silly nicknames had come from or who'd started using them first. But one thing she did know was that every time she heard these nicknames called, she felt instantly irritated. Not only did she dislike the actual nicknames, but she also resented the fact that no one could reasonably decide which one they preferred to use, and apart from anything else, she hated needless indecisiveness! While one sibling would be yelling out 'Naane!' Another would follow suit seconds later with 'Naare!' And moments after that, someone else would shout- 'Naanay!' And so, it went on. Each time, she imagined little flies, annoyingly buzzing and whizzing around her ears and taunting her for her attention. Flies, which continually escaped her deadly clap of hands and seemed to follow her around everywhere she went. She decided *that whenever the next opportunity presented itself, she'd rise to the challenge and assert herself- once and for all!* (Well, at least regarding this small matter, in any case!) And with that one final clap of her hands- all those pesky flies would finally be zapped!

Her quiet demeanor often fooled her family into assuming that just because she was smaller and appeared introverted, it was a sign of weakness. But she knew inside herself- *she was anything but weak!* Most of the time, she felt like a whole grown-up person trapped inside a small girl's body. She wasn't shy or introverted, only at certain times or around certain people. At other times, she felt positively boisterous and confident. Yet, all her previous protests regarding anything; most often seemed to fall on deaf ears or get brushed aside and dismissed as mere displays of juvenile tantrums- produced to seek attention or provide light entertainment for the others. But they'd often misjudged her. In truth, being amongst eight other- mainly larger siblings- meant that; it was not always easy for anyone to find their voice, let alone a fair ground upon which to stand. With all nine siblings growing up in constant rivalry, compounded by a shared competitive friction, there were continuous fights for that top-dog position. With all trying to outwit, outshine, and outdo one another; that delicate status quo between alliances and outsiders was constantly shifting and would often leave the smaller and quieter ones, to be picked on or unfairly overlooked, but most dangerous of all... underestimated!

DINNER SPEECH

As the day neared its end, her siblings gathered around the dinner table in their expected order of service. Having served their father's dinner first, followed by the males; it was now the female's turn- always last; to fight over the leftovers! The spicy aroma of fresh green chillies from their mother's homemade Kadhi *(yoghurt, gram flour, and onion bhaji curry)* had filled the air and stung their eyes since early morning. As Sudesh nervously folded the last few washed and ironed clothes, ready to put away, she knew the time was near- for which she'd been building up her courage all day. With their father out of the house, before whom- even her occasionally prepped up little lion-cub courage, always faltered to that of a frightened little kitten- and her brothers too, clear out of sight- it was now her perfect opportunity to make her stand before her sisters and mother at least! Eagerly listening for her call to dinner, with one ear pricked up towards the bedroom door- it came right on cue, and instantly, it was as if a swarm of flies had accumulated around her ears!

"Naareeeeeee?" Her big sister Indu screeched out from her ever-croaky throat! *(Buzzing, little flies!)*

"Naaneeeeeee?" Her big sister Satya followed suit *(buzzing, buzzing, circling her ears!)*

"Naaraaaaaaay!?" Then came her sister Prabha's call, also! *(Those damn buzzing, annoying flies!)*

Promptly arriving at the dinner table- if nothing else- to end the incessant calls, her face scrunched up like an old newspaper, she sat amongst her sisters, breathing deeply and trying to steady her nerves and watching them as they all hastily served themselves before she suddenly jumped up and startled them. Her flushed red face and apparent trepidation communally bemused them as an awkward silence took hold- in wait for her to speak.

Now, or never! She instructed herself.

"Ok then!" She'd begun assertively louder than intended- "You... all of you- listen! After today, I will not listen to anybody- if they call me by any other name but- Sudesh! Ok? Unless you say Sudesh- I'll not listen to anything you say!"

Promptly sitting down before her jelly legs gave way beneath her quivering frame and suddenly parched, she instinctively grabbed Indu's cold glass of milk and gulped it down. With Indu glaring daggers and awkward smirks chasing all the other lips, most seemed impressed by Sudesh's little- madame outburst. Yet with each millisecond feeling like an eternity; unable to wait any longer for a proper response and fearing; it might otherwise be a slap to her face- she quickly marched away towards the safety of the hallway, with a pensive expression, like that of a commanding head teacher; having just scolded her class. With her bare toes relishing the cool concrete floor as she walked, she could only breathe freely again; once she'd reached the safety of the corner wall. From behind which, she cautiously peered as her previously courageous lioness spirit; reverted to that of a frightened baby cub, and she noticed everyone return to their dinner plates. It seemed her sheer audacity to speak up; received more attention than any of the words she'd spoken. Nonetheless, days later, it occurred to her that something of what she'd said must have filtered through; as after that day, nobody seemed to call her by any of her annoying nicknames anymore. Alas, her courage had not been expelled in vain, as even when someone did slip up on the odd occasion, they'd need only clock her less-than-impressed expression to realise their mistake and promptly return to calling her solely by her chosen moniker... *Sudesh!*

GAZE

Once her father's gaze left her, she decided to esconder to the courtyard. With their lodgers busy with her younger siblings and her older siblings occupied with outdoor errands, it was a rare opportunity for her to indulge in quiet solitude. Even while most others were keen to avoid the summer sun- if it offered her respite, she didn't mind. With eight siblings, her parents, and two lodgers- the Seth household rarely offered anyone any real opportunity for an escape. The hub of activity and almost constant mayhem, expectations, and gazes; always seemed to be beckoning for something or another!

Quiet it was- for a Sunday afternoon. But only because most other sensible people had chosen to sleep through the unbearable midday heat. Most people waited for the cool early evening haze to resume their activities. With her mind drifting, she listened to the sweet sound of the birds chirping alongside the harsh interplay of other jarring noises- like loud machinery and tools or car horns; belonging to the few individuals for whom a midday siesta was simply a luxury; they could not afford! But for Sudesh, sleeping was anything but an anticipated luxury any time of the day or night! It was, in fact, a time she hated the most, always unrestful and uninviting- a time she dreaded from the very pit of her stomach when she felt lost and out of sorts and when *things* happened to her; that she could not explain or make sense of. *Things* she never spoke about to anybody. *Things* she innately knew were secret. Consequently, she did all she could to avoid sleeping altogether. Instead, managing on the bare minimum of sleep, as if merely to survive.

BUTTERFLIES

From early on, she'd imagined butterflies living inside her belly. There was no other way to explain or describe that reoccurring fluttering feeling she felt; whenever she was anxious about something or someone and something terrible was about to happen. She knew it wasn't hunger or indigestion, for it simply felt like wings rapidly moving inside her. She never talked about her butterflies with anyone or even about the terrible things they'd forewarned her. She assumed everyone had their secret butterflies living inside them, that it was something *secret*, not to be discussed. In any case, she'd got used to keeping secrets by now. Sometimes, when her butterflies fluttered hard, she imagined them exploding out of her or, worse still, being cut out of her by someone. The prospect of them flying free; was frightening and alluring at once. But mostly, her butterflies just confused her. Like so many other things in her life, which seemed to make little sense, her butterflies, too, were a mystery.

BLISS

Bliss- was standing alone in her courtyard, her eyes tightly shut, her head up towards the sky, the sun's rays kissing her cheeks, sweat beads trickling out and evaporating with the rush of fresh air.

Bliss- was extending her arms to the airwaves, her kameez top puffing up like an inflated balloon, her floral chunni scarf;

dancing meadows of flowers, her long black hair; a horse's tail on its' rampant race.

Bliss- was the picture of the horizon; as if painted inside a rising sun, with the fluffy white clouds; like snow peak mountains in the sky, or wriggling her bare toes into the scorching soils and finding the cool, moist mud buried underneath, or inhaling the scents around her and giving them a name- that algae on the riverbank, that damp moss on the tree, that freshly cut grass beneath her toes and those roses in full bloom.

Bliss- was hearing the giggling girls next door; playing or bickering over their silly made-up games, their lives a fantastic fairground, on a never-ending fun train; their playground sprinkled in laughter, surrounded by honeysuckle shrubs, and captured within their cotton candy dreams.

Bliss- was seeing their father kissing his children farewell, his faintest sweet little nothings, whispered into their ears, their giggle-filled responses; to all his silly jokes, his scooping arms and teasing tickles, his softest hushed voice- never angered or annoyed, his gracious awe, of his most precious little gifts and his eternal dedication to simply seeing them smile.

Bliss- was hearing his scooter roaring down the street, with his children's precious kisses, still moist upon his cheeks, their sweet mother calling- with damage limitation, as if held at her breast, like a rainbow appearing after a bit of rain, her velvety words of comfort and care and her sweet and savoury treats- the perfect consolation prize for any lost smiles.

"Don't worry, my angels; Papaji will be back soon. He'll bring you even more extra special treats!" her promises, always fulfilled, besides her never-ending hope.

Bliss- would be swapping her life with the giggling girls next door and wearing their beautiful newly stitched suits- made perfect in their size, dancing and skipping to that fine and innocent tune- of a childhood so melodic and harmonic that it's an orchestral dream onto itself.

LITTLE GREY BIRD

> *"I assure you that the world is not so amusing as something we imagined"* Pierre Choderlos de Laclos, 'Dangerous Liaisons'

Opening her eyes, she spotted a little grey bird perched delicately on the crumbling red brick wall- separating the two houses. It stood so proudly tall for so many years, too high to peer over and too sharply jagged to climb. Even with its edges cracked and crumbling and its paintwork all stripped and chipped, it somehow remained impenetrable and robust. Its foundations- fixed into place, as if unwilling to collapse or yield. Squinting her eyes, she tried to focus on the bird- alone, watching it stepping back and forth on the jagged edges of the wall as if it was happily dancing away upon broken glass. Chirping away, lost in its song, it seemed so blissfully unaware of all else- that was wrong with this world. Fluttering its wings; confidently, it looked like it was performing- as if for her audience, alone. She wished she could communicate with it; have it listen to all her troubles, and then take them away; contained inside a tiny parcel and tucked inside its silky wings, for deliverance elsewhere. If only she could shrink her own being small enough to fit into its wishful wings, hide in that warm, hidden haven of its soft caressing feathers, far away from the evils of this hellish place. She wished she could join it on its venturesome flight and scour the lands far and wide. Perch upon the highest hilltops. Rest beside the edges of vast seas. Explore the open terrains while cruising the waves of the wind, simply discovering life from that ever-safe distant and perfect bird's eye view. Where one could exist; untouched, unaffected, and unconcerned, and could sing and dance; unencumbered and unscathed. And she, too, would fly unbound as if she were a magical Orenda onto herself.

Flutters... It was as if fate was mocking this precious moment of sweet escapade. It was as if life's irony was a brutal hand suddenly swooning in to bring everything to a halt... when just then, a giant black crow appeared from the serene blue sky. With its broad spanning wings, razor-sharp claws, and shiny, blade-like beak- it came slicing through the cotton candy dreams. Without any warning, without hesitation or care, suddenly, it snatched the defenceless grey bird into its contorted clutches and lifted it away. The little grey bird squirmed in desperation, trying to escape, as its defenceless little cries were lost to the winds. The crow's thunderous wings clapped loudly in its glory, cawing even louder now as if proudly announcing its victorious hunt to a murder of crows.

Stunned in disbelief and unable to fathom what she'd seen, she walked towards the red brick wall and gazed up at the bright blue sky, which now, as if by magic, was fully restored to a sea of tranquility, with its snow-peeked candy clouds; so strangely inoffensive and serene. It was as if nothing had happened, as if the little grey bird had never even existed, had never sung, danced, and celebrated its short life. The merciless insignificance of its existence, its' sweet song, its final breath, just a distant whisper on the breeze, contained within the cruel mendacious calm which remained. Just then, a little whisp of a grey feather appeared and floated in front of her, straight onto her muddy feet. Picking it up, she could still feel the warmth of the body, from which it had only just been plucked, as she closed her eyes and tried blocking out that last haunting cry, which was still echoing inside her ears. Desperately searching her memory bank- back to those seconds just before, she stroked the silky soft feather between her little fingertips and tried to recall the little grey bird's ensemble. Before clasping her fist shut over the feather- afraid that it, too, might be taken away by the cruel wind. Quickly placing the feather into her kameez's (*top's*) pocket, she kept it as a little memento of the little grey bird whose memory was forever scarred by the aftermath of its small celebration and quick step to death. Yet another memory forged inside her conflicted mind, both as if fighting to leave and fighting to stay.

DOWN THE DRAIN

"Sudeeeeeeeesh!"

Her father's urgent call sliced the moment. She quickly rushed back into her house, her butterflies fluttering in a frenzy. Then, suddenly, a heavy-handed thrust hit the back of her head! The sharp, searing sting took the wind out of her breath.

"Eh! Kya kar rahe hain? *(What are you doing?)* Suna nahin? Phir se bartan dho! *(Didn't you hear? Rewash the dishes!)*."

His voice- like a blade. His commands- like bullets. His person- always abrupt and harsh. As the sting passed from her back to the crook of her neck and her voice; struggled to crawl back up into her throat, the sound barely reached her trembling lips-

"Lekin... *(But...)*"

"Lekin kya? *(But what?)*" he shouted before giving her another sharp slap to the side of her face!

Her cheek, instantly numb, quickly followed by a feeling of fire on her skin!

"Phir se! *(Again!)*" he shouted into her ear before gesturing for her to return to the kitchen.

His iron-rodded arm, and gnarly pointing fingers, always led her away from him; once he'd had his fill! Holding her cheek, she rushed towards the kitchen, resumed her crouched position by the rusty water pump, and washed her sparklingly clean dishes all over again! Her tears trickled down her face and fused her sadness into the water's slow stream. She retrieved her little grey feather and let it slip away. Watching its descent into the swirling whirlpool by her feet, she was transfixed by the spin of the water around it, like a final dance, as it momentarily gripped the edges of the grills- as if wanting to stay; while being pulled to leave. Finally letting go, its grasp relinquished; it fell deep into the drain as she imagined its descent through the veins of metal pipes, taking it on to its final resting place and, if it was lucky enough, maybe a place... a little better than here.

3

FATHER'S REIGN

"Imagine how we would be if we were less afraid"
Charlie Mackesy 'The boy, the mole, the fox, and the horse'

VOLCANO

Hearing her mother's return home, she ran towards the front door, fully intent on stealing a hug- before it was too late! They all had to fight for their mother's embrace, which was like a soft, warm blanket on a cold winter's night. Indeed, any small claim for her attention was negotiated against all the other siblings, if not just the endless wants of their ever-needy father! Those precious moments within her gaze; still fraught with her anxiety; of his impending return, subsequent needs, or relentless wants! Her mother seldom escaped, her husband's punitive vacuum state of being, and her world always revolved upon the axel of his little whims. Her attention was like gold dust. Her embrace of love, like precious stolen jewels around their neck- always hard to find and even harder to keep.

Having almost balled her over with her overzealous embrace, Sudesh relished the sweet sound of her mother's surprised little giggle, and for the briefest of moments, all else had melted away.

"Sudesh beta *(child)*... Mujhe baig tho rakhane do *(Let me, at least, put my bags down)*" Her mother coyly chuckled as she regained her balance.

But suddenly, Sudesh had been yanked away and flicked aside like an insignificant insect as her father's sudden cold hands, followed by his sternest voice, cut the warm embrace of her mother's blanket to shreds.

"Itanee der! Kyon? *(So late! Why?)*." His voice reverberated inside their ears.

Both were instantly alert as her mother tried to diffuse the situation, nervously rummaging through her shopping bags and producing a takeaway tub of freshly fried hot Jalebi's! (His favourite sweet treat!) Desperately trying to assuage him, she pathetically held them out toward him, trying to console his anger. She was well aware she was late home even if it was- merely by fifteen minutes! The money lender's doorstep had been littered with desperate wives, sharing the same expression of compromised pride, as they held out their hands in a desperate plea for mercy, kindness, and descretion, with their troubles hidden deep within their meek smiles and shrouded inside their colourful veils.

Flutters...

Jalebis- shoved back into her stomach, leaving her winded; her mother quickly turned to Sudesh and handed her the remaining bags. Her eyes silently urged her little daughter away, and her intuition screamed out when to expect that familiar little rumble of his building volcano or lockdown and prepare for his most timely eruption! Holding the crumpled bag handles into her chest, she noticed her mother's sad resignation and her even sadder, quick surrender. Her deep sighs, as if testimony; of the lack of fight, left. No choice, chance, or place for escape; her willing carcass laying itself voluntarily down, upon her butcher's table, in welcome of his axe. Sudesh looked pleadingly back at her mother, hoping to convince her somehow to fight and to do something- anything, but nothing at all! But her mother was already consumed in his shadow. She'd already turned away from her daughter's little light and, like a hypnotised disciple, stood at the gates of her hell; she'd already decided to walk through into that forever doomed place. That place, where she moved like the living dead and gave her soul to satiate the beast. As his foul breath deepened, her mother's slight breath stifled and almost seized.

"Kahaan mar gae the? Bol! *(Where were you dying? Speak!)*" His voice almost deafens their ears.

"Mai... Mai... *(I...I...)*" And before her mother could even fathom a sentence, his almighty hand had risen again! - like a leather whip lashing her skin, quickly followed by her mother's familiar little cries.

Sudesh stood in the doorway with her back turned. Too scared to even breathe too loudly, she suddenly felt a warm liquid trickle down her trouser legs and propel her feet instantly away. Fighting every fibre in her being- not to turn back and help, not to jump on the beast's back with all her might; she calmly walked away, knowing full well- that her eight-year-old body was too little a match for his! Lifting her hands over her ears, she blocked out her mother's cries, her father's rage, and that ghastly sight of hell.

Moments later, sat on the steps of her courtyard; she stared out into the open green space and wished for the outside world to consume her whole. She wished the sky could zap her into its blue sea, the burning sun could burn her being away, and the earth beneath her could swallow her into its deepest soils. *If only a little fairy's door was inside that old Ashoka tree. If only that pigeon flying over her head would let her catch a ride on its wings. If only that little rat- scurrying past her in the grass, would let her catch a sprint on the end of its tail.* Then, as the gentle breeze dried up her leak; leaving behind sore, taught salt lines across her thighs; she patiently waited for that familiar ominous quiet—that inconspicuous calm; which always came after every storm.

CLOSED DOORS

The lodgers and neighbours had closed their windows and doors. Everyone around them- so often did. Instead of calling for help and trying to protect the weak, they'd close their windows and doors right alongside their hearts and ears. They preferred to block out the bad, unsee the evil and unhear the pain. And Sudesh was too young to understand that they, too, were all trapped. They, too, shared the same jail with the same wretched captor whose chains bound them, using their fears. That same jailkeeper's keys locked them in their places and obliged them to keep quiet and keep out should they want to continue their stay and be safe under his roof. It was under his watch and control that they'd all made an unspoken pact- as if with the devil himself! For when their father was angry, there was no escape. No rhyme or reason and no negotiations- to be had. *If only she, too, could escape his gaze, block out his wrath, and unhear his hungry breath; simply by closing a window or a door.*

Finally, the ominous quiet had come just as darkness fell. She stood up, half dazed, and turned to re-enter the house; suddenly, something jumped out of the dark and scared her half to death! The almighty growl, making her scream in terror and wet herself once again; before she'd even realised- what it was! Not a wild predator or a strange monster from the dark, but a beast... far closer to home! Her very own father, wearing a dead fox's skin on his head- had come out to scare her on purpose! Just for kicks! And as he lifted the fox's skin off and laughed aloud with a thunderous, menacing guffaw, he'd instantly proven that even his measly attempts at play- were so ferociously cruel and sadistic- just like him! He was a bully- out and out! A cowardly bully who got off on terrorising the weak! She hated him even more now! Reeling from her anger and shock and with her heartbeat still caught inside her constricted throat, she ran back into the house in floods of tears as he continued to laugh and laugh and laugh!

After that, her eight year-old body and mind were forever caught in the terror of that single moment. When another part of her innocence- was taken and lost. Placing; a permanent stamp of deep-rooted terror inside her mind, her irrational fear of the dark, would hold her hostage for the rest of her life. After that day, she would never again be able to stay alone at night; after that day, she could never trust- that something sinister wouldn't jump out in the dark and take away her very last breath.

ALIEN

The lodging Sikh couple had a baby, too, and whenever she'd get the chance, Sudesh would sneak into their quarters to watch them pouring their sweet affections onto their child. Holding her so gently, they'd look at her as if she was all that mattered in the world- as if she was all that existed. It was like they'd found a magical fairy- who'd cast her spell upon them. Now spellbound, it was as if they'd gone cuckoo over her and everything she did. From the tiny curls of her soft brown locks to the fullest folds of her plump, moist skin. From the sound of her forming coos to the iridescent marbles inside her eyes. Even her tiny tippy-toes and gurgling chuckles had them instantly entranced. One minute, acting like babbling buffoons; jumping around her like wild animals; simply trying to catch a glimpse of her smile, and the next minute; tiptoeing around her and putting the world on silent to watch her peacefully sleep. It was as if they'd met an alluring alien being who'd descended from another world or planet. Enthralled by her every move; her instant devotees, from the very moment she'd been born; they worshipped her presence. As if her arrival had been foretold and as if she was a prophesied Saviour, announced in welcome by a reputed seer.

PRAY

Sometimes, Sudesh couldn't help but resent the baby and her seemingly perfectly blessed little life. It was hard not to envy such pure love and adoration; when witnessing her every little whim-attended to, her every little wish; granted, and her smallest desires-met. It only reminded her of all she didn't have, of all she didn't feel, and of all she'd never know. At times, she'd even imagine the baby suddenly being zapped back up into the sky, inside a blinding shard of light, and returned to the alien planet from which she had come—having left behind her a perfectly formed mould, like an empty voided space- which only Sudesh, could ever fill. She held fast to these images, which filled her mind with tiny glimmers of hope. Simply imagining that picture-perfect portrait of a home was like gentle kisses on her cheeks, soft stroking hands on her tired arms, and sweet lullabies upon her pillow. They provided her heart a tiny refuge, where nothing and no one could hurt her and where no sadness could remain. Where she; was the innocent being upon whom they'd all surrendered their senses and love and at whose tiny little feet they'd all come to pray.

DREAMS

"Not all those who wander are lost" J R R Tolkien, 'The Lord of the Rings'

The warm sun rays were like her mother's hands caressing her cheeks, and with her eyes still closed, she wished the day away, wanting desperately to return to her former dream- just a few seconds more. That perfect escape from reality was so intoxicating, and so clearly visible in her dreams. This time, she'd been flying as a beautifully bright and colourful bird. Alone, but not lonely. And fully alive in every way.

The sights and sounds like Technicolour- turned to full. All the animals were her friends, and just like Aurora from Sleeping Beauty, she could understand them all without ever speaking a word. The sky was her playground, and the mountain tops- her place of rest. The wonderous flowers were her sustenance and could instantly reproduce into full bloom the very moment they'd been picked. Red flowers tasted of strawberries, yellow ones of lemon curd, pink ones of candy canes, and blue ones of sherbet drops. The fresh-water lakes quenched her thirst, and everything she could see- was as if tainted by the sun. The multiple rainbows cusping the skies- were in colours still undiscovered, and the sounds of all the animals sounded like fine music to her ears.

It was a calling to a place of pure honey suckle springs. Where birds freely tap-danced, and every animal was always safe. Where darkness never fell, and terror never struck. Where her eyes always gleamed and glistened like marbled planets around the sun, and like a magical fairy, she could take shape in her fairyland in any form she chose. This secret magical place, filled with harmony and peace, was a place of everlasting love, which beamed from every soul. Where beauty was on the inside as well as on the out, but it was a beauty only ever to be found inside her sweetest dreams.

INSECT'S FEAST

Then came that God-awful sound, which sliced right through the innocence of every waking morning mood. That axe through raw flesh. That snap of a whip. That gut-wrenching sound of her father's throat-clearing ritual- plaguing each morning since she was first able to hear. A sound that made her stomach turn and brought sickness to her throat- that ghastly sound- greeting them all every single day! How she wished- *along with his disgusting phlegm; his breath would leave him too!* How she imagined his overbearing posture, collapsing like a deck of cards onto the ground, curled and cowering like a foetus in the mud and struggling to breathe; while gasping for breath. Before, those arms would fall; like dried, rotten old branches. Before they'd reach out to her, begging for help. Those bony, contorted hands- pleading for mercy. As his gurgling spit- spewed from his dungeoned mouth. And she would watch on and quietly step back and wait and observe. From the farthest shadows- tamed and unintrusive, barely there- just how he liked her and wanted her to be.

Before that final wait was over, that ominous quite returned. An absolute calm after a last storm. Finally, those eyes- still and unseeing. Finally, that hollowed-out chest- empty steel without air. Like a shell of an old bomb, left to rust and decay. The hands that drop down with their very last thunder. And all that shall remain, is her own beating heart and her little breath, suddenly so unrestricted and unrestrained. Her little lungs- free to grow inside newly oxygenated air; filling every tiny little dark corner. Finally- The End and also, The Beginning! Darkness; self-imploded; now birthing a new star; a new day; a new sunrise of hope, as he is immersed into the deep and infested soils; taken back to the hell- from which he once spawned and claimed-'He was King!' His reign- now over, his flesh reduced to fodder and above the fresh soils- her little feet freely tap-dance, whilst, beneath her toes, the creepy crawlies rejoice a late winter's feast!

MILITARY

Another mourning had started with that all too familiar dread—that all too familiar deep-seated hollowness gripping the insides of her chest. Even trying to pull her pillow around her ears, she could not block out his incessant calls; or dampen the sound of his ever-urgent prayer bells. Summoning; his loyal disciples to his early morning prayers, he rings his bells, with increasing voracity, to amplify their fears and remind them of what might happen-should any of them be late! This terror-filled prospect, enough to lunge their bodies out of bed with the forceful vigour of an alley cat, escaping a cold bucket of water overhead! Reaching his alter at 6 am sharp! They knew better than to be late! There was never any accepted reasons, exceptions, or excuse; which could grant them a single pass. So, like a naval training base, with their father the staunch captain, he hastened to run the very tightest ship. Always orderly and productive, efficient, and robust; their discipline had been engraved and reinforced by his rod. Just like at his work; as an officer in food and agriculture, he was used to being in command; to keeping his workers crippled by fear and compliantly captive; while he forced upon all; the tenets of his beliefs.

His megalomania and control had everyone around him marching in unison to his thunderous drumbeats. And even at his alter, they'd sing ever-louder to the rhythm of his jarring bells; not a single note out of place, or a single eye, even daring to look away or into his face. It was the face of a demon dressed up in Priestly suits. A face of a ruthless dictator and sanctimonious saint whose virtuous pious was nothing but show. The mocking antithesis of his existence and his duplicitous charade, hiding behind the clasp of emblematic praying hands and behind every little prayer, ascending from his lung pits of hell. Washed, ironed, and strait-laced, his military personnel align his Elysium path, where their feet never dare tread. Their nine butchered souls silently, witnessing his facade, as his Oscar-winning performance fooled the blind Gods and this pseudo-hoodwinker chief, takes his spotlight on stage. Their nine trembling hearts, riding the tocsin clang of his bells, while the devil in disguise masquerades his truest form. With a gilded veneer, stitched from the gold dust of their souls, his peeper pierces in peripheral vision with acuity; scanning for and scrutinizing any fall, any slight slip up or err; upon which to pounce. And within this sobering awakening, they concertedly stand taller and sing ever louder in simpering faith. Holding tight to every nerve; within their erected- stone-statured stance. Cursed by Medusa's glare, they brace in perfect poise. And after the prayers, they scurry away one by one; quickly onto their designated tasks, like a busy colony of ants; all diligently appeasing their Queen. Working away as part of a well-oiled machine, yet still just insignificant cogs; inside their father's giant gold wristwatch.

PRECIOUS

She rushed towards the kitchen to start washing the morning dishes—her monotonous routine caught inside the familiar few simple steps. First- to tie up her long hair into a bun. Then, to roll her salwar trousers to the pits of her knees. Then crouch down beside the rusty water pump and then start each mammoth wash! With such a large family, the dishes sure did pile up! And no sooner would her attention be taken by the ever-beckoning kitchen window, where she'd always imagined a far better life awaited. Searching the sunlight for any form of life, she'd trace the carefree footprints on the paths leading away. With the water puddled at her feet, she was snapped out of her daydream. Something was caught inside the drain bars and was blocking the water's flow. At first, she'd assumed it was a dead insect or a tangle of hairs, but then she realised, it was that same little grey feather- she'd washed away the day before. Pumping more water, she tried drawing it out before plucking it into her fingers and placing it on her small palm. Holding it towards the sun's rays, she waited for it to dry and resume its former shape when its matted fibres would return to that soft silky form. It curled and spun a dance as she watched in awe, instantly recalling that little grey bird. She decided to keep it! Looking around the bare kitchen, she spotted a little silver trinket box- once housing her mother's expensive saffron spice, which was now too costly for her mother to restock. It would make the perfect little home for her feather. She hid it deep under her mattress, knowing, even though to others, it might be a worthless and most insignificant thing to keep; for her, it felt almost magical and far more precious than even saffron itself!

4

UNANSWERED PRAYERS

"There are years that ask questions and years that answer" Zora Neale Hurston, 'Their Eyes Were Watching God'

TORN

She woke with a heaviness inside her eyes and a fuzzy feeling inside her head. Her pelvis and thighs ached with a strange burning sore sensation. She could feel the cool air rising between her legs as she descended her bed. Searching with her fingers, she'd found her salwar pants- had, yet again, been ripped. Confusion filled her mind, alongside some strange, disturbing images, and so, she quickly decided- *it must have been another bad dream!*

Perched on the edge of her bed, she stitched her torn salwar pants as her mind wandered again to that unassuming place. A place that continually pulled for her contemplation, a place she didn't want to be or see. But just then, like a lightning bolt to her mind- it came to her in a sudden flash! Suddenly she remembered; suddenly, she realised, that inescapable truth...

It was not just a bad dream!

Her butterflies fluttered in quiet chaos as the sharp needle unexpectedly pricked her finger, and a blot of blood appeared on its tip. Sucking her finger until the blood stopped, she shook her head, trying to dislodge the unsettling snapshots flashing in her head. But after a moment, she looked at her fingertip and felt an unexplainable compulsion to squeeze more blood. That sight of red paint, that sting of pain, as if bringing her the strangest relief.

TOY BOX

Her mother had taught her how to stitch from age six. She'd always loved looking at her mother's colourful cotton threads- neatly lined up, ordered in unison, and perfectly placed inside her mother's prized sewing tin. Whenever she noticed her mother taking her sewing tin out of the kitchen cupboard, she felt an instant rush of excitement, as if a magical toy box was being opened for her to explore. The sparkling ornate thimbles, the rolls of rainbow threads, the cute little pin cushions, bobbins, silver needles, and scissors were like objects out of a doll's house, alongside the array of little buttons- which looked like precious gems. It was a treat for her eyes and her imagination, and it always fascinated her; how an often plain and unassuming piece of fabric could be so expertly transformed. Simply by being cut, shaped, and stitched together using such thin threads; into something of so much more substance and use. Like a whole new piece of clothing made from old curtains or a patchwork quilt made of leftover pieces of cloth. She could watch her mother sewing for hours and never feel bored. Watching those Lego-like pieces coming together like a puzzle, with all the edges lined up and matching and everything part of a whole new thing, was almost magical to her.

Keen on perfecting her sewing skills, she made for an excellent student seamstress, paying close attention to her mother's every word and stitch and watching her meticulous hands and fingers in awe. Although her mother's stitching was perfect, her own lacked precision and the experience to compete. Nonetheless, it was the rarest of opportunities to be alone with her mother and have her undivided attention. Which sure wasn't something to stick her nose up at! For it was the only time they could legitimately sit and bond together, even if simply over a few cotton threads— these special stolen moments, like being enraptured in a utopia and finding golden nuggets of joy along the way, were often the very highlight of her day.

Over time, her hard work and attention paid off when her family could barcly distinguish between her mother's sewing efforts and her own. Soon, they were all bringing her their ripped clothes and unstitched items to fix and mend. And each time, she'd skip in excitement towards the kitchen cupboard and retrieve her favourite toy box- her mother's sewing tin!

SURREPTITIOUS

Later that day, while her mother was out shopping and her siblings were occupied elsewhere, she was alone in her room sewing, as her heart skipped a beat upon hearing a familiar and most dreaded sound- her father's crunching sandals approaching her room!

He sat beside her as her paralysing fear took hold, and her antipathy screamed from inside- knowing; what was to come! She coughed loudly, but as usual- to no avail; it failed to alert anyone's attention and stop him in his tracks! Within seconds, she felt herself starting to disappear...

Their eyes never met, and she kept her eyes closed. She always imagined his eyes were black holes that led to an endless abyss. From which no light could ever escape and into which; all is swallowed up whole. His infinite darkness, consuming everything!

Sometimes, when she'd spot her mother getting ready to leave home, she'd suddenly start acting unhinged, almost as if possessed! Doing all she could to delay her mother's exit, if not wholly thwart her leave, she'd purposefully act naughty and disruptive and start to cry, scream and beg her mother- *Please don't leave!* Even if it meant getting a firm beating and telling off, she preferred that- to the alternative, awaiting her! But her mother's reaction was always the same; just a confused look of wonder and intrigue, as if unable to comprehend the truth—her spirit- too pure to fathom the actual reasons for her daughter's sudden outbursts. Much like the others, she too had assumed- a more manageable and logical explanation- *that her daughter was simply a bad apple and a spoilt naughty brat! She did these things for attention and to stir trouble in the home!* Her superstitious mind, even wondering- *had her daughter been possessed or cursed by black magic and become a victim of 'the evil eye!?'* Indeed, there was an evil eye, seeking her daughter into view and a mutual curse, which had befallen them all, and someone most unsuspecting; had given their soul; as if possessed! But it was certainly not her daughter!

If anything, her daughter was the antithesis of what they'd all assumed, and if anything, her daughter was just too *good*... for this rotten *bad* world!

PRAYERS

> *"What we want most is only to be held and told that everything is going to be alright"* Truman Copte 'Other Voices, Other Rooms'

Endlessly confusing questions; had probed like daggers inside her mind. How unbelievable it seemed- for her mother to always be so devoted in prayer and faith, someplace else, while right here, inside her own home, the devil himself reigned! She'd often wonder- *Why had God never answered any of her mother's prayers? Why did her mother waste so much time praying to a God; who could not even hear her?* Sometimes, in her desperate attempts to console herself, she'd make up her own explanations for things, trying; to find logic and reason and negotiate her torment, and her imagination became her refuge, helping her find a little escape. Conjuring such dramatic images- like mini-movies playing inside her head; she somehow kept a lid on all her pernicious, festering hate; and kept it from exploding out of her from within...

Mother must pray elsewhere, upon- holier ground far from this horrible, hellish place! Her endless prayers and devotion; are her sacrifice for us- for herself and me. There must be so many others like her and others like me—so many others praying too, all at once, all around the world. Everyone begging for help from the same, unhearing

God, calling for his attention and help, crying for his mercy and love. Heaven must be so far away, at least far enough from this awful place! It has to be a kinder and purer place where he must live. Maybe that's why God can't hear us. He's too far away, way up high, beyond where our eyes can see, and our hands can reach. That must be why they all must hold their heads and hands up to pray and chant so loud and ring their bells with such deafening force! God must live beyond the endless skies, the cotton candy clouds, and deep within space- too far to hear and see. And the clouds, too, must muffle the sounds—of the millions of voices; all calling out at once. And maybe God hears; how I hear at night, everything muffled, strange, and unclear. Distant whispers and echoes, barely making any sense, and everyone's cries, folded into one.

But one day, he shall hear. One day, he shall come when all the millions of prayers have stacked up and formed a giant step ladder- which is tall enough to reach him and tall enough for him to descend when finally, he'll come down—taking one step after the next; answering one prayer after the other, until all steps have been climbed down and until all prayers have been answered, and until finally, he reaches my step and answers my prayer. I have to be patient and wait for my turn. Like a good little girl, I must stay quiet and wait.

For when he comes He will bring his unshakable wroth and his most unforgiving rage. He will sweep up this dirty, filthy place with one big sweep of his gigantic Godly hand and make everything new and clean again- just like it once was. Before, evil filled any heart and whispered into any ears. Before the holy became unholy, He'll deafen the evil ears, shatter the evil tongues and tear away the sinful flesh. He'll crush the evil fingers, and set them alight inside a giant fireball and extinguish them to nothing more than dust. Dust- so finite, you *can barely see it's even there. Dust- so insignificant; it can easily be blown away... even if only by a little girl's breath!*

5

'PROPER GIRL'

"If I speak of myself in different ways, that is because I look at myself in different ways" Michel de Montaigne

BLOOD

She'd been feeling unwell for over two weeks. Assuming she was merely suffering from a common tummy bug, her family had collectively self-prescribed her a vast array of ayurvedic and herbal remedies while trying to alleviate her symptoms by making her drink copious amounts of fennel and Ajwan water, milk with fresh turmeric, and making her eat fresh ginger and black pepper with spoonfuls of isabgol *(psyllium husk)* mixed into sour yogurt. Yet nothing seemed to be working! As the days passed, her family became more and more exasperated and perplexed, as her father became more and more concerned with the prospect of medical bills- should he finally give in to calling for a doctor's help? Despite no precise diagnosis, she was, nonetheless, expected at all early morning prayers- regardless of whether she'd slept. Neither was there any let-up on her expected chores. Even if she completed them, recoiling in pain and barely able to stand!

That morning, when her father's prayer bells startled her awake- having barely slept a wink; she was again greeted by the same nagging pains that had plagued her for weeks as she winced to the edge of her bed and felt a warm liquid leaking between her legs. Assuming she'd wet herself, she peeled the bed covers back and was shocked by the sight of blood! - all over her salwar pants and on her mattress, too! Instantly frightened, she lunged out of her bed as more warm liquid trickled down her legs, and when she looked down, she found even more blood puddled at her feet, like a well of death! Her first thought was- *Oh No! I'm dying!* Swiftly followed by her second *Oh No!... What a mess!* As she bolted towards the bathroom to clean herself up, planning on returning and cleaning the mess she'd left behind- before prayers finished and anyone noticed anything!

Like many humble Indian households, their family toilet and bathing facilities were outside the property. They consisted of a steel-sheeted enclosure, with holes in the ground for drainage and a single bucket allowance for bathing- using the singular cold-water tap. With no proper roofing, it was a nuisance whenever it rained and was bitterly cold outside, yet at least it helped ventilate and provide some scarcely available- privacy! With her family all busy with morning prayers, she threw her blood-stained salwar over the edge of the enclosure door and hastily cleaned the blood stains off her legs. Still, naively hoping she might make it before the end of morning prayers and somehow sneak her way into the line; without being detected. She decided she'd rather endure a good telling off- for being a bit late; than contend with a thorough beating- for missing the prayers altogether! As she watched the water flow away from her feet, in its pink, reddish colour, she desperately prayed- *Please God! Don't let me die! - Not yet!*

She hoped the blood had now stopped, and there'd be some logical explanation for it being there in the first place! Suddenly, she was startled by her mother's voice on the other side of the enclosure door.

"Nareeee! Ooooohhhh, Nareeee! Nikhaal pent- uper se! *(Move the trouser from up top!)*." Her mother's voice sounded panic-stricken!

"Nareeee nahin! Sudesh bolo! *(Not Nareeee!... Say, Sudesh!)*" She protested- as if that was the most pertinent thing at this present moment! "Mumma- Kerthi hoon! Abhi finish nahin kiya! *(I'll do it! I'm not finished yet!)*" she hollered back.

"Maine kya kaha? *(What did I say?)* Sudesh! Abhi- issi vaqth! *(Now! This minute!)*"

Her mother clearly meant business! Sensing the urgency in her voice, she quickly pulled her blood-stained salwar pants off the top of the enclosure. Stumblingly opening the door, she looked at her mother dumbfoundedly, as her mother glared at her with a strange expression.

"Satyaaaa? Erreh oh... Satyaaaa?" her mother then called out in the opposite direction; before Satya also appeared quickly, as if sensing the urgency in her mother's voice.

"Shuroo ho gaya! *(It's started!)* Satya, Ise le ja *(take her!)* ... Samaja de! *(Explain it!)*" her mother checked behind her as if afraid of someone overhearing.

What has started? Sudesh wondered- as her half-naked body continued to drip water and a little blood onto the floor. Then, without another word, she was instantly marched away into the bedroom. Before Satya discreetly opened the cupboard, took out some old cloths, and handed them to her.

"Ok, just put these inside your underclothes!" Satya nervously whispered as she pointed to Sudesh's vagina!

"Huh!?" Sudesh looked at her, bewildered!

"Look! It will just bleed a little from there... just a few days- every month! Just use these, and when fully soaked up, wash and re-use- bus! *(that's all!)* But... don't tell anyone or show anyone- anything! Hide these under your mattress!... Haaaa...! *(Yesssss...!)* I see now why you have been feeling sick recently. But don't worry; it happens to all of us... girls! It is natural..." she continued, nudging and winking at Sudesh; "Oh-ho! Nareee baby- not no baby, no more! Now, you are- a proper girl!" Satya teasingly said before skipping away and leaving Sudesh even more confused than before!

TRINKET BOX

She lifted her mattress to hide the spare cloths and noticed a small trinket box buried deep beneath it. Reaching in, she pulled it out, wondering *what it could be and why it was there?*

Flutters...

Oh no! She suddenly thought- *Maybe, it's Black Magic! Maybe, somebody put it there on purpose- to curse me! Perhaps, this is why I'm bleeding?* Suddenly terrified, she threw the trinket box across the bedroom floor. She knew better- than to risk handling it too much and had instantly decided- she needed to dispose of it- immediately! Coming from such a superstitious family and community, she'd heard enough stories to sufficiently scare her-half to death, about such things! Anything related to voodoo and black magic had always given her the creeps. She didn't even like hearing about such things, let alone discussing them! Apprehensively walking towards it, trying to get a closer look, she noticed its lid had come away, and something strange had fallen out of it. Her heart skipped a beat as she inspected it a little closer and realised it was, in fact, a little grey feather!

Huh...? Why would anyone use such a strange thing- like a feather, to curse me with? She wondered.

Just then, a slight draft came rushing into the room, taking the feather away from her as she hurtled forward, trying to catch it. But, just missing her grasp, the feather flew into the air, heading straight towards the window, before being taken through the little gap. She watched on, following its ascent towards the bright blue sky, as it floated higher and higher; before completely disappearing out of sight. A strange feeling came over her. It felt like an anticipation and a relief, quickly followed by the most bizarre sense of calm...

And suddenly, she remembered!

Like an instant flash going off inside her head- she'd seen a memory come flooding back to her and instantly recalled- what it was and where it had come from. That distinct memory of the little grey bird, singing and dancing upon the red brick wall- from all those years ago; was followed by the awful memory of the black crow. Who'd suddenly swooped in and snatched the bird into its sharp claws; taking its very last breath. Leaving the haunting sound of the little grey bird's distant cries; echoing inside her ears all over again.

CHANGE

Indeed, change was in the air...!

Spring was dawning, with the onset of snowdrops, daffodils, and violets; all bathing courageously in the rays of sunlight, and right before the canopies of the green-shaded Banyan trees; could fill like a forest above them and start to block out the sun.

Besides the onset of bleeding every month, her body seemed to have changed too. Her clothes were now tighter- especially around her chest and hips, and she'd started experiencing erratic feelings and impromptu emotions and found herself caught in the strangest contemplations. However, the most significant change was that she no longer woke up with strangely ripped salwar trousers. And somehow, she could now sleep right through the night; without being disturbed. She had fewer nightmares and could now recall more pleasant dreams more vividly and often; her dreams felt more immersive and filled with new wonders. She was no longer consumed with relentless confusion and doubts or continually questioning- what was imaginary and real? She'd stopped begging and pleading for her mother- *to always stay home* and instead, relished those little moments, left home alone. Yet still, never happy to be left *alone in the dark!* No matter how many other things had changed, and seemingly for good, her irrational fear of the dark continued as an exception to the rule! And although the wild beast; still lived amongst the little cubs, his vengeful attacks spared more moments in between- when the little cubs could discreetly reclaim a few more nuggets of joy and peace.

FRIENDS AND FOES

"I could fit in anywhere, yet I belonged nowhere"
Christie Aschwanden 'O's little book of happiness'

All nine siblings inevitably clashed at some point during their childhood. Their Alliances and rivalries were constantly being forged and broken over the slightest disagreements or umbrage over the silliest things. While some clashed in their heterogeneous personalities and habits, others got swept into one another's feuds. With the tides always turning- on who'd be the next victim- of the clan's collective assault, each newly homogenized pack would shift again. Although on the surface, they'd all obediently bow down their heads before their leader; they still secretly plotted against other comrades- behind his back. The subtle tensions, always interplaying beneath their simmering smiles, with each wanting to exert some power and control, if not simply exorcise, some of their pent-up frustrations.

Often, they'd find themselves unintentionally mimicking their father's dysfunctional traits and repeating his toxic patterns of behaviour, and it seemed that even the most innocent and passive ones amongst them; could not entirely escape the negative imprints of their father's emblematic seal. Even if it meant finding more subtle and secret ways to put up their fight, they'd-innocently hide under the radar- like wolves in sheep's clothing, having learned from the master manipulator himself! And all had some experience; of being the insider and the outsider, being liked and disliked, being protected and unprotected, and all could relate to those familiar territories, which held them enslaved, nonetheless.

Even while forging their individual personalities and slotting into their pre-conceived roles, the shifting hierarchy within the status quo; provided a little window of opportunity to reshuffle the deck or reconfigure the pieces in this endless game of chess. Most often, it was unclear who the winners and losers were; or who amongst them; were mere pawns in someone else's game!

SAVAGE SATYA

The greatest sibling rivalry, blighting Sudesh's childhood, was between her and her eldest sister, Satya! Although her elder sister; Indu, too, often stoked her fiercest fires; it was Satya's physical attacks; which proved most traumatising and brutal of all. Not only the eldest female but the heaviest one, too; she took every opportunity to utilise this fact! If not, incessantly teasing someone about their appearances and abilities, she'd sit on top of them and crush them beneath her! And for some unknown reason, she was intent on Sudesh getting the brunt of it! First, she'd catch her alone. Then pounce on top of her and tackle her to the ground. Then pinning her beneath, she'd start to pinch and punch her incessantly, continuing; until Sudesh would either stop crying and admit complete surrender and defeat or wet herself! Understandably, Sudesh was terrified of her almost as much as she was of her father! And so, she did all she could to avoid being around Satya, especially alone! Even when it meant hiding away for hours or staying clear of the house, whenever she'd spot Satya in her midst, she'd instantly be on guard, knowing it was just a matter of time before another attack was imminent!

ADORABLE AMBO

"We are all in the gutter, but some of us are looking at the stars", Oscar Wilde

During her early childhood, Sudesh didn't have many friends. Mainly as a direct consequence of her father's strict regime, but also because she wasn't as confident around strangers. Yet from the moment she'd set eyes upon Ambo (short for Amarjit) in her first class at school- their connection was instantaneous. Like they had an affinity and had always known one another, with both wishing- they were real sisters and wholeheartedly believing- they simply must have been in a previous life!

Ambo came from a poor Sikh family. Living; alongside the other more impoverished families- who were ostracised from the richer ones- on the road opposite their own. The girls would sneak in playtime whenever they could—each day, meeting at the same street corner- which divided their streets and very different lives! Walking; the two miles to and from school together and stealing moments together to play in the alleyways and courtyards surrounding their homes. On occasion, Sudesh would even sneak in a short visit to Ambo's house, where she was always welcomed with open arms and offered kind treats, even when this courtesy couldn't be reciprocated. Sudesh's family had forbidden their affiliation from the start and made it crystal clear that- 'Poor girls like Ambo; were not to be trusted and not to be welcomed in their house!' Their father shared a seemingly popular warped perception- that poorer, lower caste people were fundamentally thieves who used black magic against wealthier, higher classes, only serving to marginalise families like Ambo's even more within society.

Ambo carried a continuously bewildered expression upon her face, and in many ways, she was, in fact, in awe of life, of people, and all things. Her observant, curious nature- like that of a prowling cat and unique way of expressing things, was often surprisingly entertaining to all those around. Refreshingly honest and unfiltered, yet rarely unkind, she'd notice the silliest, most minor things and find it impossible- not to comment upon them. Usually, saying something- that most others were thinking; but daren't ever say out loud! Her long black hair, which extended beyond her backside, swayed like a horse's mane when she walked, sweeping floors as she trotted along. Forbidden to ever cut it- due to her strict Sikh faith; she wore it greased down in a couple of plaits, perfectly finished off with a colourful parandi *(fake hair extension)* matching the colour of her dress. Mostly seen wearing humble salwar kameez suits, she was like an authentic Punjabi doll, with warm olive skin, constantly flushed cheeks, and naturally blushed lips, which made her appear as if entirely made up. Her deep-set, dark eyes always seemed to smile, even when sad, and her perfect little button nose would instinctively twitch when thinking. If not, scrunch up like a rag whenever she'd laugh. And laugh she did, almost constantly! Her laugh was so contagious that it made everyone else laugh too. Even without knowing the joke and even when it wasn't appropriate to do so! Ambo loved pulling silly faces and mimicking people's voices. Yet it never came from a cruel or unkind place, merely from a place of wanting to have fun. And fun too- she indeed had, constantly! Fun surrounded her like an invisible magic cloak, and that same fun- pulled others in wherever she went.

"Look, look how that man's hairs- are all standing up to attention!" She'd snigger, or "Look, how bent this carrot is?"

Her apt coruscating way of putting things- marred with her cheeky humour; had always set her apart. Indeed, Ambo could find humour in almost anything. Even within those moments when one is expected to be mature and serious! Like once, when in class, a priest had come to lead morning prayers, and she'd caught sight of his long gnarly toenails!

"Oh, meri maaa! *(Oh, mother!)* Look at those toenails! Like dead centipede on his feet!" She whispered into Sudesh's ear, sending her into instant fits of naughty giggles.

It was as if Ambo saw life through invisible fun spectacles, even on the saddest and dreariest days; her lenses seemed to search for rainbows and silver linings. Even when unwell, she had such a way of playing it down. She was like a lamp in the dark, a bright star on the blackest night, and the essence of joy as if personified. With her glass always full- if not overspilling! - She could flip the switch on sadness anytime, anywhere she went, unknowingly creating nuggets of joy effortlessly as if it were synonymous with her breathing. Taking every opportunity, the girls would secretly meet and ride their bashed-up bikes around their neighbourhood and play silly made-up games using scavenged old junk. And it certainly didn't seem as if Ambo's lack of money, lower caste, or the fact that she lived on the poorer side of the street- had any bearing at all on how good, kind, or trustworthy she was, let alone affect how much fun, she could indeed have!

MOVING

"Memories warm you up from the inside. But they also tear you apart" Haruki Murakami

Having lived in old Delhi since birth; when their father suddenly informed the family of eleven- that they'd be moving house the following week; needless to say, they were surprised and upset. Being uprooted from their formerly larger home, alongside giving up all the open land and outdoor space surrounding it, only to go and live in a significantly smaller house- with no outdoor space- certainly seemed nonsensical! Even while the move was to a more desirably affluent position in New Delhi. Yet again, their self-serving father's vanity and want- to outwardly display his socially aspirational image; superseded any of his family's choices, comforts, and convenience.

But for Sudesh, it was the thought of leaving Ambo; which hurt the most. But there was also this strange melancholic pull; of leaving her childhood home and local haunts, which confused her. The familiarities of home, no matter how grotesque and twisted, were nonetheless yielding. Now aged fifteen, she looked back on her past with mixed conflicted feelings, which often collided and surged within. Her childhood felt both evocatively alluring and anchoring and as if something which she hankered after and yet simultaneously, filled with such devastation and despair. Those hauntingly traumatic snapshots, etched into her memory box, although hazier beneath the webs of passing time, still had a strange hold of her. Right on the cusp of adulthood, she was already navigating a host of new changes within her body and mind and was only just at the very precipice of finding herself;

before suddenly feeling like she was being uprooted, untethered, and marched on!

As she said her final goodbye to Ambo; knowing deep down inside herself- with the geographical distance dividing them- things could never be the same; she nonetheless smiled and agreed to keep contact and nevertheless promised they'd write, phone, and even try to visit. Genuinely believing that someday, somehow; they'd both be reunited again. Yet, it was the first time Ambo's eyes hadn't smiled back and the first time she was in her company- devoid of fun. Sadly, that romantic notion of a friendship being everlasting would remain just that- a notion!

And fate would give their friendship another harsh blow; just a short time after leaving, Sudesh discovered that Ambo had been married off to a perfect stranger! Aged just 16 and shipped off to live in Haridwar with her new adopted family, in an instant, life had pulled the rug out from under her feet and instantly quashed any former ambitions and desires. And knowing Ambo, this would likely have been devastating! It broke Sudesh's heart, simply imagining such a vibrantly spirited girl like Ambo, having to live a quietly stifled, shrunken life with the wind sucked out from beneath her sails, her fun spectacles ripped off her face, and her shining halo dimmed, alongside its illustrious light. Now burdened beneath her newfound obligations and commitments, the abrupt cynicism of life would have so harshly zapped her out of that innocent cocoon of carefree childhood. Those days filled with the chase of fun; would be replaced by days of monotony, chores, and obligations. And indeed, once the excitement and fanfare of her wedding were over; she'd quickly have realised- like so many other young girls before and after her- that she never stood a chance; that her choices were never hers, to begin with, and from the moment she'd arrived- unwanted, unappreciated, and unloved- having taken the fateful place of a much-preferred male- life was already stacked up against her and her happiness. Ultimately, she'd realise, others decided her fate, made her decisions, steered her ship, and played the tune to which, like all other girls- she'd be expected to dance!

Alas, with no contact number or forwarding address, Sudesh could not trace her dear friends' footsteps and would never see or hear from her again. Still in their teens, as they'd both swiftly turned to bid one another that giggle-filled farewell, neither had realised it would be the last time they'd set eyes on one another. Had Sudesh known, she'd have hugged Ambo just a little tighter. She'd have studied her smile a little longer, and before cramming into the back of the family truck, she'd have stopped to tell Ambo- *just how much she loved her, how much she'd miss her and her laughter and her silly games- the sweetest anecdotes in life and she'd have made sure Ambo knew... she was pure magic!*

SERIOUSLY SINCERE SANTOSH!

Santosh lived in a property behind Sudesh's new house, close enough to see one another from their windows- if not converse over the dividing fences. Officially having met at the local Punjab college to study Metric (equivalent to GCSE and O-Levels)- once they'd realised that they lived a stone's throw away from one another, it seemed a given to commute to and from college together and to buddy-up for studying. Even though, like Ambo, Sudesh's family resented her affiliation with Santosh, who was also from a poorer and lower caste family. The eldest of her two siblings, Santosh was respected and treated almost like a second mother in the home. Often relied upon as the sole carer to supervise the younger brutes while their mother and father were away working. Yet even though she rarely complained of juggling the pressures of studying with her other responsibilities, Sudesh could tell that she sometimes resented it even when she tried her best to remain calm and composed, smiling through her gritted teeth, simply observing her younger siblings' immature shenanigans! Although, for Sudesh, the younger sibling's silliness was entertaining. It reminded her of that occasional silliness; she'd once created with Ambo and would never recreate with anyone else.

Santosh was a high academic achiever, and her general demeanour; though far more serious than that of Ambo; was still warm and welcoming. Although the expression on her face often made her appear much older and wiser, if not slightly intimidating, she was a gentle spirit underneath. She also wore her long dark hair in two well-greased plaits, finished with a traditional hair parandi- just like Ambo and mainly dressed in traditional Punjabi salwar kameez suits- just like Ambo. But their similarities started and ended there. Unlike Ambo; Santosh's feet were firmly on the ground, and she had little interest or patience for pointless pursuits or meaningless procrastination- and if Ambo were the open sky; then Santosh was the stabilising ground beneath. It seemed a sure given; Santosh would make something of herself academically and in her career prospects someday. Luckily for her- with no intentions of marrying her off young; her family fully supported her, and any of her dreams and Sudesh always imagined, they'd lead her to become a respected schoolteacher, a politician, or maybe even a doctor. Envying her home life, she'd observe her with her loving parents and siblings—their home, as if cultivated with an abundant light of love and warmth.

Santosh's mother was not only an accomplished cook; but also, a frugal home keeper. Besides enjoying feeding people- at every opportunity she got, she also had a knack for taking the humblest of left-over ingredients and turning them into something special. Never one for wasting, she'd even take left-over vegetable skin peels and turn them into delicious, deep-fried snacks, a stew, or soup; if not, pickle them, and she'd found an ingenious and cheap way to wash dishes, using a unique mixture made with mud. Which, during water shortages- seemed an incredibly sensible idea! While there, Sudesh would happily join in, and without realising, she was further antagonising her family; she'd come home and suggest that- '...they, too, all start washing the dishes using mud!'

At Santosh's house, Sudesh never heard anyone raising their voices, let alone arguing and fighting with deep-seated hatred! Alongside constantly trying to fatten Sudesh up, they'd shower her with affection and compliments. Occasionally, even cook her favourite curry to entice her secret visits.

"Toshi! *(Santosh)* Tell Sudesh- to come and have her favourite- Kala chana! *(Black beans curry)* I made it, especially for her! Tell her to come to devour it- nice and fresh!" Santosh's mother would holler from her kitchen.

Her father, too, was a complete contrast to Sudesh's and would always excitedly announce her arrival at the front door, as if he was welcoming an honoured V.I.P. guest or celebrity!

"Oh, ho! Ah gayee! Ah gaee! *(She's here! She's here!)*." He'd cheerfully announce.

Loud and proud, he'd consistently demonstrate his love and pride in all his children, whether male or female! He was the type of father; she could only ever dream of having. One who needn't raise his voice or beat his wife and children half to death- just to assert his power and control and who needn't terrorise them, just to maintain their respectful obedience or desperate fear of him!

FOREVER FRIENDS

"Life is what happens while you are busy making plans" John Lennon

During these pivotal teenage years, Sudesh and Santosh's friendship flourished. Sharing school and social times, and even occasional sleepovers- aptly disguised as study nights, they were almost inseparable and, like most other teenage friends- also believed; they'd remain best friends forever. Forever, caught inside this same bubble of carefree camaraderie and expecting to share life's many ups and downs, as if it was them; against the world! Like so many best friends before them, they, too, had envisioned their futures carved out side by side and bearing witness; to one another's victories and defeats, imagining all those first-time experiences; they'd get to share.

That first-ever courtship, that first-ever kiss- with mutual best friends, maybe even brothers! Those cute little foursome dates and becoming bestie Brides someday! - supporting one another through all the fun marriage preparations, like picking out Bridal gowns, wedding jewels, and wedding gifts and teasing each other's fiancés at all the ceremonial events and moments filled with jest. They'd even planned on getting pregnant together. So, they could both get fat simultaneously, eating mounds of endless cake! And having picked out their children's names, they'd decided to have-two boys, followed by two girls, promising- their kids, too, would grow up as best friends.

They imagined pushing their prams around the park and having messy toddler play dates, family dinner parties, birthday celebrations, and even foreign family holidays together, creating all those picture-perfect memories as if in Technicolor print. And someday, in that far-off future, they'd imagined themselves basking in the midday Sun, sitting on an old park bench. Their friendship galvanised, like the steel rods beneath their seats, having stood the test of time. Reminiscing on their fortunate and blessed long lives; now greyer and older, with walking sticks at their sides; they'd watch their grandchildren playing upon the newly refurbished swings. They'd compare their childhoods, ever convinced- theirs was the best! And relive many melancholic memories inside their fuzzy fickle brains. While trying to reconcile their heavy nostalgic hearts- they'd both shed a few tears, hankering after that past, and both realise- that time waited for no one... not even them. Now left with but a single hope that they would not be forgotten and that their life stories, too, would be passed on and remembered- generation after generation. Hoping their legacies lived on long after they were gone, like precious family history books made of anecdotal tales, they'd still have enough energy to bicker over;

"...which one recalled their story correctly, and which one-told it best!"

6

E = MC 2- Squared

"How sad and bad and mad it was- but then, how it was sweet" Robert Browning

RESULTS

It was results day, and Sudesh was waiting with bated breath as a searing anticipation for the morning's newspaper to arrive had her eyes firmly fixed upon the front door. Her sweaty palms clasped together upon her lap, and her being; fully braced, it was as if she was awaiting an impact. Yet she was too scared to tempt her fate by announcing the expected post, so she kept her lips sealed. Not even realising, most of her family were already privy to the importance of today's mail and their nonchalance; was merely a guise to hide their shared worry for her fate. Knowing how much these results meant and how hard she'd worked, though they'd never openly encouraged her educational pursuits, they nonetheless sympathised with how much she wanted to prove herself. Not least to herself and them, but most importantly, to her cynical father; whose belief in her; was always overshadowed by his prejudice against girls studying- in the first place! Luckily, he and his critical opinions, were both absent today!

She'd already envisioned jumping up in delight and running about the house, hugging each person she saw and announcing her good news. There was always a marked difference in their demeanours; when their father was away. Like a dead weight had been lifted off their shoulders, like warmer and lighter air had been permitted into the otherwise stagnant, dull place within which they'd usually coexist with their father's forboding presence, which had them all on tender-hooks. But in his absence, all their steps seemed lighter and less hesitant. Their laughter seemed to echo more loudly throughout the house; they moved, a little free'er and could all speak, more at ease. They needn't worry about what he might see or hear, and with no immediate consequences to anything, breathing more freely itself was a luxury!

Upon hearing the familiar footsteps of the postman; heading closer towards the front door, she ran, hurtling towards him; as if a firecracker had gone off behind her! She flung the door open, startling the postman, and, before he'd even knocked, snatched the newspaper from his hands. Firecracker- as if still in pursuit, she ran off with the newspaper, tightly clasped inside her sweaty armpit.

"Offo! ...Oh! Sudessssssssh!" Her mother grimaced, instantly embarrassed by her daughter's rudeness and walking towards the postman; both rolling their eyes, as if in agreement- *of how incredibly spoilt today's youths are!*

"Aajakal ke bachche! Ooff! *(Kids nowadays! Oh my!)*" the postman mumbled, shaking his greasy bald head and calmly walking away as her mother closed the door behind him.

Crouched down on the floor around the living room corner, she scrambled to the newspaper's back pages as her eyes darted side to side in pursuit of the series of roll numbers allocated to her year's class. Her mother appeared by her side, holding a dishcloth and steel bowl in her hands and meticulously rubbing it as if it were a genie's lamp- to which she quietly made her wish. Trying to act calm and uninterested while quietly hoping and praying at her daughter's side- for good news, she, too, waited with bated breath. Finally finding the series of roll numbers close to hers, she scanned for her personal roll number, besides which she would go on to find a single, most powerful word. One would pat her on her back and propel her education further upon its trajectory, and the other would stop her dead in her tracks! Her eyes scanned on and on, past the annoyingly small-font numbers, as her heartbeat pounded hard inside her chest, and she finally found her roll number. Then moving her finger away, her heart skipped a beat as she gasped in a sharp breath and noticed the last word she wanted to see! ... 'FAIL!'

Blood suddenly drained from her head and her face, suddenly numb, her eyes instantly filled with tears; as she looked again and again through her blurred vision and checked and rechecked to be sure- she wasn't misreading something or accidentally stumbled on some other unfortunate student's results! But no matter how much her mind protested or how often she checked that final verdict remained the same! Indeed, she had failed!

Her mother feebly crept away from her side, trying to act unperturbed, as she continued polishing her steel bowl, her

Genie's wish- unfulfilled! And her attempts to act sensitive, by not further upsetting her daughter and drawing unnecessary attention to her failings, had instead achieved the opposite effect! Now Sudesh felt as if her mother didn't even care! The feeling of disappointment; so palpable in the air, set alongside the pity inside her mother's deep sighs; only adding to her misery.

"Maths! Mumma... Maths!" She proclaimed- "I can't believe- I failed cause of Maths!"

She hoped for some reassurance, some words of comfort and solace, anything but the ignorance of her mother's utter silence! Then, screwing up the newspaper angrily and tossing it aside, she marched off to her room in a childish strop—the disgruntled injustice; etched across her tear-ridden face! Aged sixteen- these results were pivotal for enrolling in a college course and majoring in a chosen subject. But now her hopes were diminished by that one word, which continued to ring inside her head like a doomsday clock!... Fail! Fail! Fail!

TRAINING

"It was as if, by setting to rights the externals of her world, she would be able to rid herself of the chaos within"- 'Whatever happened to baby Jane' by Henry Farrell

All females had been continually reminded that a girl needn't concern herself with education or waste time and energy trying to achieve a career, for she'd seldom reap any of the rewards. Right from the moment she was born, she'd already been preordained and predestined into an ordinary life of servitude and domesticity. But still, this did not alleviate Sudesh's deep-seated disappointment and dismay. She was aware that most people believed; a girl's main prerogative was to become a good daughter, a good sister, a good daughter-in-law, a good wife, and ultimately, a good mother. She was aware that most other females; were expected to be married off; at a young and tender age; to a perfect stranger found by their family. One who was specially selected; based upon their family's credentials, class, social status, financial standing, and reputation. She knew most females were simply transferred from one family's responsibility; to another's, that her sole purpose was to keep her house and home, to keep honour and respect, to maintain domestic order, and to attend to her family's every whim and want. Her primary obligation and objective; was to prolong a family's bloodline with the successful births of more males!

Yet, accepting such limiting hopes and dreams didn't feel like enough. Simply residing to such a primitive and sole purpose, even if all the others had, wasn't enough! At least, not until she'd tasted something more; some freedom, hope, aspiration, a dream-something! Marriage looked like a life sentence, from one prison to the next. It seemed to cancel all other ambitions and goals and stifle any other hopes, like shrinking to fit in, like apologising for having a bigger dream. To repeat the same limited life cycles; she'd seen repeated so many times before- as if caught inside a slowly strangling noose, which invisibly and inevitably suffocated you- was not her idea of living life! She wanted something beyond that expected and apparent space and the quiet pain and suffering she'd witnessed inside her mother's eyes. More than just that pitiful acceptance of fate, which she'd seen projected in the eyes of so many other older females, she knew. Those pasted on, quivering- little smiles covering such pain. Those forced little chuckles; beneath veils of shame and suffering. That shared disappointment, those fear-ridden steps, and that shared longing... so heavy with all the *what if's...?* There seemed to be too many compromised hearts, hands, smiles, and wombs surrounding her. And she could not help but wonder;

What else might lay beyond those compromised souls? What other space they may have occupied- were they ever given a choice? What was beyond the confines of a well-stocked pantry, an overused laundry room, an endlessly re-lit chulha-stove, and a nursery- filled with more spoilt spoon-fed boys? What other voices could be heard; besides the infantilising tones; so often used to appease so many full-grown men!?

INDERPAL WILKU

"Synchronicity is an ever-present reality for those who have eyes to see" Carl Jung

Inderpal Wilku (Inder) was twenty-four and lived in the house directly opposite The Seths with his parents, two younger sisters, and one younger brother. Good friends with Sudesh's older brother- Raj, Inder's younger sister too, happened to be friends with Sudesh's older/rival sister, Indu. Tall, with a medium build, he had warm eyes and a confident, approachable, and dis-alarming demeanour, which bode well for him in social settings. With a knack for engaging with people; regardless of their education, background, class, or age, and although he'd failed to get his proper respect- as the eldest son within his household; he was nonetheless popular, affable, and well-respected by all his peers. Charming, educated, and knowledgeable, he also took great pride in his appearance, almost as expected of a naval or army officer. Although, this was not for reasons of vanity or from being forced into a strict regime; but merely a reflection of his graceful discipline and tidy elegance. He had- what one might class as good habits and good manners. Always clean-shaven, even his shoes were kept squeaky clean and highly polished enough- that you could see a reflection in them and his neatly kept hairstyle, always worn perfectly set to one side of his head, gave him a geek chic like appearance. Primarily dressed in traditional cotton Indian kurta pyjama suits- finished off perfectly with his waxed and ironed Nehru style- jacket, or else dressed in a crisp English gentleman's suit, his dress sense was a cross between an official looking Indian M.P and a young Shaun Connery- from a Bond movie and often giving him the appearance of an elevated social ranking and status- which in truth; far superseded reality. Indeed, Inder liked to make a good impression wherever he went.

Often popping in at The Seth's house to visit Raj, together with his impeccable manners and warm, friendly personality, he'd quickly and most effortlessly been accepted into the folds, and, like another son, he was openly offered food and drink; without formalities or hesitations. Aside from the lodgers, he was the only friend permitted regular welcome and access within The Seth's otherwise private home. But, most surprising of all, he'd unwittingly won over the most stringent clan member and, like all the others, their father, too, had succumbed to Inder's delicate charm offensive while also falling folly to the strangest- *nice spell*; whenever Inder, was around!

FOOD STRIKE!

He momentarily stopped, just about to devour the freshly made aloo paratha *(pan-fried chapatis stuffed with potatoes)* beneath a generous dollop of ghee *(purified butter)*. Having noticed Sudesh hadn't even greeted him today. Seated right opposite him, she seemed unusually quiet and withdrawn. Whilst all the others were already onto their second helpings and thirds, her plate and favourite food sat barely touched under her nose, and her attention seemed as if a million miles away. Even when he leant in towards her, her gaze remained firmly fixed beyond his left shoulder. With their father away, it wasn't often the clan could forgo their strict mealtime regimes. So how bizarre it seemed to him- *for Sudesh to deny herself a taste of those glorious golden discs, flying freshly off her mother's sizzling hot pan...?*

As their mother entered, holding a large platter filled to the top with her final batch of parathas, she was almost balled over by her overzealous children! All were excitedly diving in to grab the freshest ones off the top, eagerly jostling and laughing. Making the most of their father's absence and that rare feeling of being free. All except Sudesh! Who nonetheless remained as if a million miles away...

"Oh, Inder!" her mother suddenly noticed his distraction- "... uhhh... uhhh... Narreee sad today! Failed igzhaaam! *(Exam!)* ... Mathmatic, nor- nor pass!" her mother suddenly blurted, alongside a slight snigger and shrug.

Her attempts to make light of the situation annoyed her daughter even more! And besides her careless insensitivity, her big mouth, too now, left Sudesh feeling embarrassed; as she glared daggers at her. *Inder! Of all people! She goes and tells Inder!* She thought, feeling increasingly wound up- *that intellectual brainbox- would no doubt be an even harsher critic of my failure than most!* And she could imagine what he might be thinking- *...how dumb Sudesh must be not even to be able to pass such a little basic exam!*

She could sense his eyes on her, with a mixture of pity and scorn, and could almost hear his mind ticking over, trying to find an apt response. Knowing him, likely to be another silly quick-witted joke- testimony of his feeble attempts to make light of the situation and dissolve any awkwardness at once. But she had no interest in his opinion or silly jokes on this occasion! As far as she was concerned- *it was none of his business, and her mother had no right- to divulge her affairs to him! Please, God, don't let him say a word! Let him eat his food and go and take with him; his clever comments, smug face, and ridiculously shiny shoes!* She prayed, having clocked his shoes by the door. But after a moment, he surprised even her. When he loudly cleared his throat and said the most unexpected thing!

"Chalo, tho! *(Come then!)* Until she will eat...I, too, will not!" And with that, he gently pushed his plate away.

"Oh-ho! Inder nor, nor!... eat food, pleeeeeze?" her mother pleaded, gently pushing his plate back in and turning her eyeballs on Sudesh!

Now feeling even more embarrassed and somewhat irritated- by what seemed like Inder's patronising attempts to disarm her into submission, she sensed the rising stakes! Made to feel like a silly child having a meaningless tantrum- she was now faced with a new conundrum. Emphatically sighing and duly noting- how gracious her mother was to encourage Inder to eat- yet barely batted an eyelid about whether her daughter followed suit! She suddenly felt her mother nudge her shoulder while continuing to glare. As if she was silently imploring her- '...stop all this silly nonsense at once and just eat your food!'

Her mother's strangely nervous smile, filled with warning and spread-eagled across her face; although alarming, was easy to ignore. And with her siblings preoccupied with their dinner plates, the tension continued to mount between them in this silent stand-off. Yet still, she stubbornly resisted and ignored her mother's silent pleas, audaciously determined not to give in! Even when the seductive aromas permeated beneath her nostrils and teased her for a slight taste! Soon she'd realised how stubborn Inder could be, too! Without another word, he eased his plate away as the pressure became almost unbearable!

But as much as she hated- admitting defeat, she finally relented and pulled her plate back in. Signalling her cooperation and hoping her little gesture of compliance- would prove enough to spur Inder on. But Inder was undoubtedly no fool! Demonstrating his strong will, he mimicked her and patiently waited until she started eating! Finally, she lifted the tiniest handful of parathas and plonked it unenthusiastically into her mouth. Before reluctantly chewing it through her gritted teeth, even if the explosion of saliva wonderfully welcoming in the taste- clearly suggested otherwise! Then, looking audaciously into his face, she exaggeratedly chewed her food- with her mouth wide open, unashamed in her contempt; as her mortified mother looked on, helplessly shocked by her daughter's rude display and still nervously smiling! But ever cool as a cucumber, Inder smirked; before he, too, finally started to eat his food!

Her mother's loud sighs of relief filled the airwaves! Revelling in his quiet victory, Inder picked up the pace. Suddenly acting ravenous, he chewed faster and faster until he'd reached a comical crescendo and had the whole table in uncontrollable fits of laughter, all except for Sudesh! Looking stubbornly unimpressed, she held fast to her serious expression. Only making them all laugh even more as she continued to fight every fibre in her being. Even while the tension around her was plucked out of the air and replaced with lingering laughter, she was determined to make her point!

Although, in truth, it had long since escaped, even her; *what* that point... ever was!?

7

TERE GHAR KE SAMNE (OPPOSITE YOUR HOUSE)

"Excellence is the gradual result of always striving to do better" Pat Riley

TUTOR

After attaining a high-honors Math degree, Inder worked full-time as an Architect at The All-India Radio station alongside his father. Yet still, days later, when he'd gallantly offered to start tutoring Sudesh for free; to help ensure she passed her maths retake exam- it had come as a surprise, especially to her! Considering, just days earlier, she'd behaved so rudely and immaturely in front of him. Nonetheless, when her family questioned Inder- about this generous offer, he'd rather sweetly responded- '...it was his way of thanking them for their kindness and for treating him like family.'

Knowing they'd be hard pushed to find Sudesh a private tutor- one they could trust and two- afford, it took minimal persuasion for all to agree, including Sudesh's father. Who'd always sought the cheapest, if not free option, in everything!

Considering Inder already had a full-time job, Sudesh knew that he'd be sacrificing his valuable spare time- which might otherwise be spent relaxing or pursuing hobbies. Realising this, she felt guilty for her previous behaviour, for not showing him due respect, and for misjudging and underestimating him. Now, she had little choice but to pass her retake exam with flying colours, especially now that more people were vested in her passing. Under this extra pressure, she'd now have to ensure she avoided letting herself down as well as her new *private tutor!*

RIVALS

It was common knowledge that aside from Inder and Hema's friendships with Sudesh's siblings, their parents weren't keen on one another. In fact, often, they'd purposefully avoid each other, if not pretend to have not seen one another, while out and about. From the outset, they had a strange and unsaid rivalry running between them, of which no one knew the origins. Although they didn't encourage their children's affiliation- with no real and valid reason to stop them; they could neither openly object. Besides, asserting any apparent divisions was too awkward, with Inder coming over so often and being delightful. For Sudesh, the two hours of studying away from home; even just across the street- was a welcomed little escape, not least from her endless chores but also from her father's unwanted attention. Besides, she enjoyed learning and was still determined to use her education to help her make something of herself. At least, a little more than they expected!

PREPARED

Expected; to commit to two hour-long Math sessions each week; it was also agreed that the sessions- should be held at Inder's house. Given that he already had a study room ready and set up, it further pleased her family that she'd be nearby and in safe, trusted hands. As her first scheduled Math lesson approached, she took a little extra care to look presentable, given that Inder himself always looked so well-turned out. She expected that even within his home, he'd likely be just as meticulous about everything. She prepared her book bag to ensure she had all she might need- so as not to inconvenience him in any way further. Her mother had already coached her, on her expected conduct, while in Inder's home-

"Samay par aaen aur jaen. Achchhee tarah se padhaee kerna. Sabhee se achchhe se baat kerna aur bahut jyaada baat mat kerna! *(Come and go on time. Study nicely. Speak nicely with everyone and don't talk too much!)*."

Although her mother's hypocrisy hadn't escaped her, knowing that their parents didn't even bother to acknowledge one another, let alone worry about appearing respectful! - she was wise enough to appreciate that there was one rule for the parents and another for the kids!

As she walked towards Inder's front door, a strange nervousness overcame her, and her butterflies took flight in anticipation. Unsure how she'd be greeted or by whom, she quietly prayed for it not to be his parents, or worst still- his sister Hema!

SOUR FACE HEMA!

Inder's sister Hema had been unusually strange around Sudesh from the start. Besides having one of those miserable resting faces- which always made her appear angry, cold, and unapproachable; she also refrained from making eye contact with Sudesh or even greeting her properly- when she'd see her. If Sudesh tried to make eye contact or start a conversation, Hema would always snub her and pretend; she'd not seen or heard her. Else, she'd answer abruptly and shut down any conversation. Sudesh had no idea; why Hema acted like this around her and couldn't fathom any real reason or cause for her coldness towards her. Yet it was always there, like an unsaid truth. It seemed as if Hema had instinctively taken a disliking to her, for no reason, right from the moment she'd first met her. Although Inder and Hema had visited Raj and Indu at Sudesh's house many times, this was the first time she'd go there alone. The prospect unnerved her and made her palms sweat profusely; struggling to grab the handles of her schoolbag upon her shoulder- she tried her best to remain calm beneath her pasted-on and forced smile.

FRONT DOOR

Nervously checking behind her- to ensure none of her neighbours was snooping- she was aware of how quickly and easily; idle gossip could spread. Like wildfire in a forest, it simply took one wagging mouth to light that match! Making a concerted effort to look respectable, she pulled her chunni scarf tightly around her body and checked it was still, modestly covering her chest. As she approached his door, she found herself wrestling with sudden gusts of wind, stinging her skin and annoyingly lifting her chunni scarf off her body! Quickly placing her school bag in plain sight- in front of herself; she tried to signal to any prying eyes; that her visit to the house opposite was purely for studying purposes. Although she felt silly being so paranoid and knew full well, she had nothing to hide, her instincts were rarely wrong, and for some strange reason, today they were screaming toward caution. Now with her butterflies fluttering in a frenzy, she was taken aback by the sudden face which greeted her from behind the front door. Just her luck- it was Hema- stood there, without so much as a polite- 'hello!' and looking at her dumbfoundedly. Suddenly self-conscious and awkward, Sudesh tried to muster her voice, to speak!

"Oh... Umm... Hell... hello... Hem... Hema... In... Inder... is... he... ho...?"

But before she could finish her sentence, another sudden wind swooned in and unexpectedly yanked her chunni scarf straight off her chest! Now, with her bosomed cleavage- fully exposed, she noticed Hema's beady eyes fixated on her chest! She grappled with her scarf, trying to cover herself back up again. Then, exposed and embarrassed, with her face suddenly turned red and hot, she again attempted speaking. But her voice remained stuck inside her increasingly dry throat!

"Uhhh...Uhhh...Uhhh...!" She stammered on.

Seemingly enjoying, making Sudesh squirm; Hema continued to stare as if revelling in this strange power game. Sudesh meekly smiled back, hoping it might break the ice between them... but it didn't!

"I...umm...Inder...umm...?" Sudesh stuttered nervously again.

Just then, and to her great relief, Inder finally appeared from behind Hema!

"Eh...! Hema!" He suddenly called out, "Let her come! She is here for tuition! Let her in!"

His commanding voice surprised them both. Sudesh had never heard Inder speak so assertively before. Hema looked on, clearly unimpressed, before reluctantly excusing herself as if dragged through water. Then, snidely bowing her head down in an exaggerated welcome, she signalled Sudesh to enter. Her scathing sarcasm, as biting as the winds outside! Hesitantly entering, like a little mouse, into a lion's den, Sudesh continued, nervously smiling as she followed behind Inder and as he gestured for her to come through to the hallway and into what seemed like the main living room area. She could still feel Hema's eyes piercing into her back as her breath remained caught inside her chest. Not until she'd caught a glimpse of Hema walking away towards the kitchen- could she finally breathe again! Other than Hema and Inder, it seemed like no one else was home, which was both a relief and slightly unnerving.

▨ MESS!

Inder's house felt uncomfortably hot, like an oven had been left on. Although Sudesh was more than relieved to be away from the biting winds outside- it was still so unexpectedly and stiflingly hot; that she could barely catch her breath. She noticed a familiar smell of musky sandalwood incense sticks and a distinct hint of some strange soapy scent, as if someone had spilled talcum powder all over the house. Yet, although the house smelt clean- it certainly didn't look it! Surprisingly, there was mess everywhere! The house, too, seemed smaller than Sudesh had anticipated. Or maybe, it was just the fact that there was such an overbearing mound of clutter and junk accumulated all over the place- like an internal landfill; which made it seem that way. With barely any space to walk, sit, or even stand, there appeared to be stuff everywhere. From piles of odd-bod objects, bits of clothing, and left-over fabrics; to empty boxes, half-used bottles, and tubs, random nick knacks occupied every nook and cranny as if fighting for space. Things were stacked and piled over one another so haphazardly; that it was difficult to ascertain where any furniture was placed or where the floor space began and ended! Sudesh was surprised, especially given that Inder was always well-kept, organised, clean, and tidy. She'd assumed his home would reflect him, and with three women living with the three men, it seemed especially strange to find such domestic discourse. If she didn't know otherwise, she'd have assumed burglars had ransacked the place, or they were clearing out for a complete renovation! Instead, it was quite the opposite- of how she and her family lived. Indeed, had her house ever been left in such disarray- especially in front of visitors; their father would likely have skinned someone alive- starting first with the females- for having dared to negate their most primal duties!

With hardly any light coming in, the dark grey cement walls appeared stark and unloved, as if they were pushing in over the space, slowly suffocating its inhabitants. The cracked, chipped ceilings and walls, with their pealing layers of old paint and left-over bits of wallpaper, looked neglected and left to fade and flake away over time. A separate kitchen sat off the main room, and a small study room was adjacent. There seemed to be another little room beyond the kitchen, assumingly some larder, where Sudesh also spotted an outdoor stairwell, which she presumed led to some upstairs quarters. The house felt as unwelcoming as Hema's sour face, and just like her face, it too lacked any signs of light and love. The few pictures of the various Hindu Gods were barely hanging on display and clinging haphazardly and unsymmetrically from the crumbling walls. Dirt and grime stuck on the edges of the photo frames and any care with which they may once have been selected, framed, and mounted; was but a distant echo of a former pride, like an ancient and precious relic left in the dorms of an old museum. With the glory days past, history lays dormant and hidden behind the clustered cobwebs of time. Sudesh fought hard to hide her growing expression of disgust under her meagre smile. She waited for Inder's next cue. Unsure whether she should stay standing, try to sit down, or walk anywhere. Instead, she remained awkwardly frozen in her spot, sensing Inder's embarrassment by his pitiful surroundings. He shuffled in his spot before finally ushering her into the study room.

SPOTLESS STUDY

She spotted Inder's brown leather shoes neatly placed outside his study room door- as if signalling the entrance to his personal domain. Finally, she felt reassured and calmer from her otherwise braced being. His shoes were like the crowning glory of his Alladin's cave and entrance into a far more welcoming and warmer space. She was instantly struck by the stark contrast- of his organised tidiness and the pristine condition of everything inside- especially when compared with the chaos just outside! Although it was a small space, every inch had been carefully thought out. As if with consideration for its best use and just like Inder, it not only presented well and seemed organised and tidy; but also felt like it somehow belonged elsewhere.

Inder pointed for her to sit on one of the two wooden chairs, the only pieces of furniture inhabiting the small space alongside a small wooden desk and bookshelf. A few, nicely framed certificates, were symmetrically lined up and mounted upon the freshly painted, crisp cream walls, proudly displaying Inder's many academic and sporting achievements and the glass upon the frames, so squeaky clean that she could see her reflection in them. Light bounced off the walls from the single little window, pointing to the side alleyway and perfectly catching the few rays of early evening sunlight. Even the small paper bin looked clean, with a fresh, empty bin liner. The matching wooden desk and bookcase were varnished, showing off their rich, mahogany wood tones to their fullest effect.

That's more like it! She thought to herself, clocking the neatly piled stacks of papers, books, and folders; perfectly matched in size order; with no spine, out of place! Reluctant to touch anything in case she messed anything up, she could instantly tell; Inder was a stickler for details! Just then, they heard the annoyingly loud sound of stainless-steel dishes and cutlery- being roughly handled in the kitchen. Of course, it was Hema! - purposefully trying to be disruptive and intent on making her presence known. Clearly annoyed, Inder rolled his eyes to the back of his head and shook it side to side; before suddenly launching towards the door as if about to slam it shut. Stopping momentarily- after noticing

Sudesh's slight flinch, he, instead, courteously left the door ajar, as if making a concerted effort to show respect- for having a lone female in his company.

FORMALITIES

She noticed a stark difference in Inder too. Instantly more serious, refrained, and almost formal. Even though at her house, his manner was quite the opposite. Always warm, cheerful, friendly, and carefree. Yet here, in his own environment, where she'd expected him to be even cooler, even more relaxed, and as the eldest son- lauded over by all the females- he was instead as if emasculated and from the moment she'd first walked in, it was clear that *something* was amiss here...?

"Good, you came on time; I have other work after this," he told her as he lifted a sizeable thick Math book from the pile of books at his desk.

"Oh...achcha... *(yes...)*", she replied, clocking the tall glass filled with perfectly matching sized- sharpened pencils.

"Ok, let us start!" he snapped, abruptly plonking the heavy Math book before her and unintentionally making her flinch again.

Then, smiling feebly, she reached for her bag to find herself a pencil. And before she'd even opened her case, he'd already produced a perfectly sharpened pencil under her nose. At times, Inder's reticent manner seemed formal and somewhat impatient. She quickly realised he had no time to waste on small talk or idleness. Fleetingly reminding her of her father, he leaned in and explained the Math's work, just as she picked up on that same soapy talcum powder scent, once again, permeating off his chest.

Then, a further loud clunking of dishes; startled them both! Before he sighed deeply and again rolled his eyes to the back of his head. Nonetheless, despite all the annoying racket of noisy pots and pans being handled, they continued their lesson, with him simply speaking a little louder and she; simply listening more intently.

8

SHIFTING

"People are sent into our lives to teach us things, that we need to learn about ourselves"

Mandy Hale

PUPIL'S PROGRESS

Inder was a focused teacher, and Sudesh- was a diligent pupil. She'd found she was learning more in the two hours of tuition than she'd learned in her whole year at school! The one-to-one guidance and keen focus- did wonders for her confidence and ability to grasp the learning. Before long, she excelled beyond her simple pass mark expectation grade, and her progress was unquestionable. She'd whiz through the Maths homework- which he'd set her each week and eagerly await her next lesson; to further impress him with all the correct answers. Like an excited puppy, she'd gleefully watch him tick the answers- one after another; as if he were giving her mini pats on her back. Over time, Hema, too, seemed to have given up on purposely being disruptive. To Sudesh's great relief, Inder started answering the front door to her, saving her from any unnecessary awkwardness and rather thoughtfully, he'd started leaving her a fresh cold glass of homemade lemonade on the desk- as if preempting how hot she felt in his house and how ever-thirsty she seemed. And soon, he even started leaving a biscuit beside her lemonade- on the off chance she was peckish.

STRANGE

The winter sun shone brightly outside, and the fresh air filled her lungs. She could feel the sun kissing her face as a gentle breeze swept between her billowing dress and lifted it around her like an inflated balloon. Home alone, the small communal green patch at the back of the property was often the only quiet and peaceful spot for a bit of escape. She indulged in this moment of calm bliss before contemplating the prospect of getting ready and going to her tuition. She was battling the increasing temptation to forgo it- just this once so that she could enjoy this moment a little longer; she looked at her wristwatch- now reading 5.50 pm. But her calm indulgence was quickly replaced with her racing, anxious heart and fluttering butterflies amongst that niggling little voice inside her head, which probed like an irritating insect, intent on ruining her plans!

You couldn't possibly not turn up!' It buzzed away! *'...You couldn't just leave Inder there, waiting for you! How very ungrateful, even to consider such a selfish thing! After all, he has done for you! After all, he's sacrificed! Do you want to fail all over again?*

6 pm sharp, her reluctant knuckles were knocking at his door as if on autopilot! As the door opened, she forced on her trademark smile to hide her disinterest.

"Hello!" he greeted her energetically.

"Hello..." she replied before sighing deeply.

As she entered his annoyingly messy and stiflingly hot house, her weighted feet thudded towards his study room, all the time yearning to step back again in the opposite direction. Back, towards that satisfyingly cool breeze; back outside- right there- right outside the front door!

He closed the door.

His family were all out and likely enjoying the warm fresh evening's air elsewhere. Like so many other sensible people and like- she wished she could! His perfectly polished shoes sat unusually back to front today, outside his study...

Strange... she thought.

She took her books out, feeling a slight nervousness creeping over her. Inder, too, seemed less relaxed today. *Maybe the heat was finally annoying him too? Or maybe, he'd had another argument with his family? As he so often did!* Her butterflies fluttered with a strange expectation of something... something... and then she noticed... no lemonade...? No biscuit...?

Strange... she thought.

Something felt different today. But she couldn't put her finger on it. It was more than just the missing glass of lemonade or biscuit- something else felt amiss today. She could sense Inder staring at her as she prepped her workstation. She wondered for a moment if she had something on her face. Then she wondered if maybe Inder was gearing up to give her some bad news like- 'I'm sorry, Sudesh, but I'm afraid I can no longer teach you!' or something to that effect! Her mind raced in confusion as she shuddered and wondered if Inder might tell her off about something! 'Sudesh, I am disappointed in you! You got the answers in your last test sheet all wrong! I'm not happy with your progress! I can't help you anymore. I'm afraid- you're just no good at Maths... I don't think you'll pass; your retake!'

But instead... instead... he stepped in strangely close to her, and just as she turned to face him, their eyes suddenly locked... and then... then... their lips! She froze! Barely able to breathe! Time, as if stopped!...

Why is this house always so, so annoyingly hot!? Her mind was suddenly shouting inside her! Unable to move, speak, even breathe freely; she felt as if a lightning bolt had gone through her entire body, as she quickly forced her eyes down to the floor- lacking the courage to look up again... lacking the courage to look at him again... ever, again! She noticed his bare-naked feet, clenching the floors beneath... *he had nice feet.*

What the Hell! A voice suddenly screamed inside- *What the bloody, bloody, bloody Hell!!!???*

She wanted to run away- a million miles away! Then, grabbing her belongings in sudden haste, she bolted out of the room as fast as her feet could carry her, bearing in mind her legs were now weak like jelly, and her heartbeat was pounding like thunder inside her chest- the loudest thunder ever! With sweat dripping from her forehead, alongside the sudden onset of unexpected tears- she ran back home.

REFLECTION

When she arrived home, she went straight to the bathroom and stared into the small mirror on the wall for what felt like an eternity. She couldn't recognise herself, and her face seemed suddenly so alien! Her trembling hands held tightly to the edges of the sink, desperately keeping her numb legs from giving way beneath her. She felt like she was drowning, drowning in the plain air!

Oh my God! What the hell did he go and do that for? Her mind shouted, *surely, he must know- he'd be killed? - if anyone were to have seen him? Seen us! If anyone ever found out what he did to me!*

She couldn't bear the thought of seeing him ever again! She was confused, angry, nervous, annoyed, frustrated, embarrassed, overwhelmed, and somewhere amongst all those mixed feelings, she also felt strangely shy and silly too... as well as a whole lot *stupid!*

AVOID

> *"...A moment when the memories of the past collided with the realities of the present"*'Whatever happened to baby Jane' Henry Farrell

She told no one. She thought it was *bad,* and felt it was wrong. For two long weeks, she hadn't turned up to her math tuition, and when quizzed by family, she'd make excuses about not feeling well, that Inder was unwell, or simply busy with his work and commitments. All the time, praying no one would catch on and call her out on her lies, force her into going back to his house, or worse still- discover what had happened between them!

As the days and weeks passed, her excuses became strangely repetitive and increasingly unconvincing. She knew it was only a matter of time before someone's suspicions were raised, and she'd find herself being questioned and scrutinised more. She knew she had to think of something- fast! She tried her hardest to avoid Inder whenever entering and exiting her house, having to endlessly check from the window first before leaving. And on return, stopping around the corner to ensure he was nowhere in sight; before she'd dart to her front door without looking up, even for a second! Luckily, Inder, too, had refrained from coming over to visit with Raj, and she couldn't help but wonder- *whether he, too, was purposefully avoiding her?* She was left with so many frustrating questions to which she knew she might never get any answers. Like, *why had he done that? Why had he ruined everything? What did he think- would happen?*

With no sight of Inder for weeks, she wondered *if he'd fallen out with Raj over something?* But she couldn't bring herself to ask Raj! Shuddering every time anyone even mentioned Inder's name, every day was now spiked with dreadful nerves, anxiety, and the relentless replaying of the scenario- of what had happened! Playing on repeat inside her mind, she found herself thinking about it- almost endlessly! And as hard as she'd try to distract herself with other things, her mind would continually return, *there* again! Right back to that very day and that single moment- there in his house; in his study- stood face to face- his soft lips upon hers... when *everything* seemed to have changed!

HOLY-SIGHT

She often attended prayers with her mother on Tuesdays at the local temple. As is the case for many Hindus- Tuesdays are considered the day of Lord Hanuman (The Monkey God). Traditionally a sacred day of the week, many Hindus and some Sikhs either fast or abstain from eating meat produce and often partake in special, commemorative prayers.

She'd not seen Inder for almost three weeks now and had almost forgotten what he looked like; his image now- a million miles away. But one thing she certainly hadn't forgotten was his *lips!* And how they looked and felt- placed upon *hers!* It was her *first-ever kiss* and was now etched into her mind forever. With her butterflies all aflutter, she was increasingly nervous whenever she left her house and went anywhere. Endlessly afraid of bumping into him, she knew it was only a matter of time before she'd finally see him. Living right opposite her and being such good friends with Raj, it was only a question of when? When would she have to face him again?

As she approached the temple grounds, with her mother at her side, she suddenly remembered that Inder, too, had previously mentioned; *how he'd occasionally attend this very same temple on Tuesdays for these very same prayers!* Suddenly she realised he might *actually* be there! Infuriated with herself- for not having recalled this information sooner; she knew it was now too late to turn back home. She'd have to pray- even harder! - *he wasn't there on this day, had already left, or would arrive once she had exited!* Although, with so many people around, it was difficult to find anyone specific- at the best of times, in the large crowds of people, and likely easier; to lose someone! Still, that slight possibility of seeing him, even at a far and safe distance, filled her whole being with dread! Luckily for her, thus far, there was no sign of him! And to her greatest relief, the usually long- two-hour prayers had already started and were close to finishing by the time her mother and she had arrived.

Phew! she'd thought as she grabbed her mother's arm tighter, afraid of losing her to the swelling crowd.

Today, she had prayed harder than ever before. She'd prayed *for a solution to this unexpected problem and a clear way out. But most of all, she prayed for some peace of mind!*

Ever since it happened, she'd felt so discombobulated and out of sorts, and her anxiety was through the roof! She'd not felt a sense of calm for so long, and her nerves had been in such tatters that they exhausted her.

As they were about to leave, her mother left her side momentarily to go and meet the pundit *(holy priest)* and collect some holy prasad *(a food blessing- often consisting of fruits or nuts)* to take home. Once reunited again, they both turned to leave, as Sudesh's heart suddenly skipped a beat, and she saw a familiar face set amongst the crowds of devotees in front of her...

It was him!... *Inder!*

Trying her hardest to avoid his sightline, she pretended not to have seen him. Quickly looking away and forcing her head down under the guise of her chunni scarf, she promptly made for the adjacent exit sign, dragging her poor and confused mother with her. In sudden haste, she was weaving her way through the crowds of people, holding ever tighter to her mother's arm.

"Offo! Sudesh!... Kya yah sab jaldabaajee? *(What is all this hurry?)*." Her confused mother cried out, trying to pull her arm back from her daughter's tightening grip!

"Mumma..., mumma please! I have to study! Let's go! Quickly! Come- quickly!" Sudesh insisted, with sudden urgency, as her mother looked at her with growing confusion.

"Offo! Vo dekho Shilpa aantee! *(Look, there's Shilpa Aunty!)*." Her mother suddenly pleaded, veering away.

Luckily for Sudesh, Shilpa Aunty had already gotten distracted and was now talking to some other gossipmonger in the crowd. Again, pulling her mother back, Sudesh tried to lead her away again forcefully.

"Agalee baar! *(Next time!)*" She insisted.

Oh my! Please, dear God! Don't let him see me! Please! Please! Please, dear God! Sudesh prayed desperately inside her head; as she headed ever faster toward the beckoning exit sign and finally sighed a huge sigh of relief, having assumed- she'd effectively avoided the dreaded encounter! But then, as she let go of her mother's arm, her mother had again spotted another bloody Aunty! - again, drifting away from her!

"Oh! Vahaan dekho, Kamal aantee! *(Oh! Look, there is Kamal Aunty!)* Kamaaaaaal? Areh ooooh *(Hey there!)* Kamaaaal?" Her mother veered away yet again- now headed towards Kamal Aunty!

"Offo! *(Oh My!)*" Sudesh cried out in frustration, "Achchha! Jaatee hoon main! Ghar par miloongi! *(Ok! I'm going! Meet you at home!)*."

Determinedly marching on by herself, she headed towards the temple steps with her head forced down under her scarf. Finally, having reached the steps, she was suddenly stopped, dead in her tracks! It was him again! Stood right in front of her, grinning, as she looked at him, flummoxed and wondering; *how he'd made it there before her!* She realised she now had few options for escape! Trying to avoid a big commotion, she spoke quickly and instinctively, in a loud whisper-

"Why...? Why did you...? I... I will complain to my brother! Do you hear me?" her confused, stuttered words fell out of her, making little sense.

Yet again, it had all come out wrong! Her nervous, incoherent mumbles left her cheeks flushed and her heart pounding. Struggling to articulate any more words, she felt childish and silly, and, with no actual response from him, bar his continually smug smirk, she quickly turned away, just about to storm off. But then, he suddenly grabbed her by her arm as another bolt of lightning; seemed to shoot through her blood-filled veins! Suddenly, he pulled her forcibly towards him. His strong hand made her instantly tense up, on high alert. For a moment- the longest moment! - he held her close- too close! - close enough to kiss, just as his sandalwood scent, followed by his warm breath, glided past her flushed cheek.

"Achchha... *(Good...)*" he said. As every tiny hair on her neck stood up, "Look, it's totally up to you, what you want to do, but you still... need to come to study..." he shrugged and calmly continued, as a sudden chill ran through her, alongside a flutter in her pelvis.

His shamelessness! His sheer audacity! Shocked her! Now, stunned into quiet stillness, she looked back at him; with the seconds feeling like an eternity; as she fought the magnetic pull towards his lips and couldn't help but feel, ever so slightly impressed- by his sheer confidence! And yet... *How dare he? How very dare he?* Fighting a sudden desire to smirk back at him, or else slap him across his face! - she was again caught off guard and unsure how to react to him or even what to say or do. Instead, she yanked her arm back abruptly and said the only word she could find and articulate-

"Fine!"

Quickly rushing away, she felt his deep silent stare piercing into her back, alongside another magnetic pull, right back towards him. And just then, as if by strange coincidence, came the loud and resounding sound of the temple bells ringing through the crowds of bodies and between her ears. Before falling into unison with her pounding heartbeat and stomping footsteps, desperately searching solid ground beyond the feeling of quicksand at her feet.

9

GENESIS

"I was within and without, simultaneously enchanted and repelled by the inexhaustible variety of life" F Scott Fitzgerald, 'The Great Gatsby'

SOMETHING...

The first lesson back was awkward, to say the least! Both behaved even more formally than before. As if conducting strict business, both seemed determined to ignore the giant elephant in the room, staring back at them- dumbfoundedly and as if in wait for *something...*

They'd naively assumed they could return to how things were before as if nothing had happened. Not even that *first kiss!* They'd continued to act obliviously, even when their very existences had been so unwittingly propelled into this strange, unknown territory. Their insides, constantly stirred, grasped within internal chaos and rapid waters, bubbled away beneath their forcibly stern expressions and dedicated concentrations. *Something* now lay beyond their absent stares and inside their hesitant beings. *Something-* always present now, no matter how hard they resisted and ignored it. And it gnawed away at them like a stinging bite of an insect, consistently requiring an itch—*something* which had irreparably changed and significantly shifted between them.

No matter how casual, normal, or formal they'd hastened to behave, it was always there, like an uninvited guest—whispering beneath their breaths, simmering inside the blush of their cheeks and pounding for their attention inside every skipped heartbeat. Every single time he would come near. Every time he'd look at her. Every time he'd call out her name... it would sting again and cause an involuntary flinch, inside and out. Without any cause or real reason, they were both in defence. Both guarded up as if ready for an attack. Ready and almost in anticipation of that... *something...!* And whenever their eyes would lock, just a millisecond too long; whenever he'd brush past her, now constantly tensed being; whenever his warm breath would caress past her skin, she would feel it all over again, that undercurrent of strange excitement and terror. That certain electric charge, searing within. That fizz- inside her hollow stomach and flutter of her pelvis. That increase in blood flow- suddenly shooting through her veins; each time, she was fleetingly reminded of that same flashing light bulb image of his lips... her lips... their lips together... over and over and over, again!

Look away...! She'd kept instructing herself! *Look away! Stand back! Look at the pages! Just keep looking at the pages!* She could no longer look directly into his eyes- at least without feeling her entire being, being pulled into somewhere else— where she could not find an escape. So, she decided... she would never look into his eyes again!

CHANGED

Now, constantly on edge around him, she sensed; he, too, had changed. He, too, battled something within. Fumbling and stumbling slightly and jarring his incoherent words in confusion; whenever he was around her. Nothing felt the same anymore. Nothing tasted the same or even looked the same anymore. Even the sky above their heads; had somehow shifted forever. Even when they both kept their attentions, strictly and most stubbornly, upon the black and white pages, they studied and worked ever harder to concentrate and focus on their tasks; still, it was never long before that image would return. When the black numbers and words; started to melt away and disappear; when an all-consuming white; lured them back in and held their gaze without release; when that white angel flashed, and it all flooded back again... his lips, her lips, their lips together and that first ever *kiss*. Now, as if; all they could ever see!

TIRED

She returned home tired. More than the usual tiredness might follow an extended school day or an intense study stint. Now, it was a tiredness, amplified by the immense amount of energy required to keep her focus and keep a watch on herself. Now, she'd become mindful of everything she said and did. Every time she was around him, she could now, never relax! Watching how she moved, sat, stood, and stared. It was knowing that anything might be misconstrued. Even an innocent smile or giggle, even a stare- a little too long; might lead him on somehow, give him the wrong idea, or create false hope. Desperately trying to maintain her composure and grace whilst every cell in her body fought against her endlessly- was itself exhausting, alongside constantly feeling as if she was caught in a tumble dryer of emotions. Pushed, pulled, and twisted in every direction; her mind screaming for rumination upon anything; *anything* but him and his lips and how they felt, placed upon hers!

Soon, even her will to keep studying; had come into question as she began wondering whether; *it was even worth it anymore? Whether it wasn't best to accept it was now ruined? Accept that it could now never be the same. Maybe she should just quit- while she was ahead? Perhaps it was best to stop her tuition and forgo her retake exam altogether?* Her mind was constantly conflicted and confused. She couldn't find any easy solution or way out of this horrible mess! Which, she duly noted... *he* had created! He had been the one who'd ruined it all! He was the one to blame for her current afflictions! And for that alone, she resented him! *If only there was a reset button. If only I could go back to that day- just before. That minute- just before and somehow, stop him! Before he ruined everything!* She kept wishing. But if she was truly honest with herself; there was also a little distant voice; deep down within herself; which continually whispered- a counterargument and continuously called for something quite contrary... her sweet surrender.

TEACHER'S NOTE

"I know. I was there. I saw the great void in your soul, and you saw mine" Sebastian Faulks

Her deep sighs travelled alongside her footsteps all the way home. As she turned to close her front door, she noticed his front door- still ajar and wondered- *Why today- he'd not closed it right behind her?* Headed straight for her room to change; it occurred to her how much more often she now needed to change her clothes, of late. She was sweating so much more now and feeling constantly flushed, when it wasn't even that hot! As she took her math books out of her bag, she noticed a piece of paper fall out onto her feet. She picked it. It was a note, reading...

'I LOVE YOU! I WILL LOVE YOU FOREVER MERI JAAN! (My love!) x'

Left unsigned, besides an 'X'- (kiss), she instantly knew- who it was from! Short, sweet, and to the point... *just like him!* Suddenly, there was a lump in her throat as she read the words over and over as if trying to soak up their ink. Half in disbelief, half outraged; she was also struck by an unexpected excitement, as well as- terror! Her butterflies- were wide awake as she stared at the white paper inside her trembling hands, and soon enough... the words melted away, and a snow angel appeared and, with it, that familiar flashing image of that first-ever kiss. Now, this too was a first for her... her first-ever love letter! Albeit- merely eight words long!

GOOD CATCH

Days later, she finally confided with her friend Santosh. To her surprise, rather than be repulsed and outraged, she was instead encouraging her! With a sudden passion in her voice, which sounded so alien!

"Sudesh rani *(princess)* True love...!" She exclaimed, "...is very hard to find! And if you have found it, why not- think carefully- so that one day, you won't regret...?" she soberly warned.

She'd never banked on Santosh being such a romantic! Her otherwise serious seeming friend's; sudden sentimentality was surprising and also slightly terrifying! It made the prospect of a courtship with Inder more tangible and plausible. Somehow, it gave the situation a rather unexpected validity, and the very thing; she'd previously ruled out was now a matter for actual consideration, like a lamp had been lit to reveal a new and unknown path. One where she could now see a slight clearing and where she'd previously only ever conjured a brick wall!

"Look. Listen to me!" Santosh wasn't done yet! "...too many girls are married without consent, forced to marry strangers- forced to live lives they didn't choose. But look! You have a choice! And... I think you should take it! Take this chance... take what you can... when you can!"

Her friend's vindication was alarming and undoubtedly inspiring! For a moment, she fought a sudden desire to burst out laughing- right, into Santosh's earnest and impassioned face. She'd never heard her speak like this. Yet her somewhat overdramatic speech, which resounded almost like a Shakespearian love sonnet, sure had some truth to it. They were words of undeniable wisdom;

beyond her years. And just when Sudesh thought- she was done, her friend piped up, yet again!

"Dek na! *(Look now!)*" She asserted, "Inder is an excellent catch! He is a perfect match!" She quickly pulled Sudesh by her arm; "...look, naa? He is clever, smart, fit, has good manners, is kind and funny, has a good job, earns good money... what more you bloody want!?" She scoffed, "...he is much better than all the other idiots, we know! Nai?" She emphatically continued.

And even though she'd started to annoy her, Sudesh realised, she was right!

"Yes... yes, that is true..." Sudesh contemplated, half wondering whether- Santosh had a soft spot for Inder! - given all her suddenly exuberant and unabashed compliments of him!

"Oh...!" Santosh jumped up again as if she'd won Bingo! "And! All your family already know him, and they already like him! So he is, in fact, the most perfect choice! What could be better than that?" Santosh declared in elation.

"Yes! But you, silly idiot fool- they all like him as my brother's friend! As my teacher! Not as my bloody lover!" Sudesh grimaced, pulling Santosh by her arm and back to reality!

Shaking her head and sighing deeply, Sudesh stared into space; as reality dawned on her more and more, just like that familiar, heavy stomping foot of her father's leather sandal, it came thundering down to crush all hope! Simply imagining her father's reaction; was enough to evoke utter terror inside her! And she realised she could not pursue it! It was too ridiculous of a fantasy! Far, far too dangerous! And no matter how exciting the *what if's* may have appeared and how carried away she'd allowed herself to get; upon the coattails of her friend's romanticising- the simple fact remained; that given their age gap, given their circumstances and given the fact, that both their parent's- pretty much hated one another- a romantic notion between them, was, out of the question and a sure recipe for disaster! She knew, without a doubt, if anyone had got heed of anything between them, there would be absolute carnage! And they would be skinned alive, just like her father's old fox's head!

MIRROR

"You are your best thing" Toni Morrison

Gazing at her reflection in the mirror, she tried to control her erratic breath. Her thoughts spun in anticipation of another hour-which she knew would be ridden with anxiety in Inder's company. Yet, looking at herself with deep contemplation, it was as if something was dawning on her for the very first time...

Many times, in the past, people had complimented her on her beauty, and each time, she'd always assumed they were being polite and saying things to be nice. She'd seldom seen what others seemed to see in her. In her humble opinion, she'd already decided- she was quite plain and average looking, with no actual defining or stand-out features to speak of. There was nothing extraordinary about her, and for all intense and purposes, she felt unbothered to waste copious amounts of precious time and energy on the endless task of beauty and vanity. Besides, she felt there were far more productive things one could spend time on. In fact, the one thing that may set her apart from the crowd was that she wasn't obsessed with her appearance or how high she ranked on the school's beauty radar list! It was of little consequence to her, yet it seemed all-consuming for many other girls her age. No doubt, exasperated by family's expectations- to use a daughter's beauty ranking as a quantifying tool to bargain with and validate her; for the best-arranged marriage matches- especially when a family fell short in other areas, like their caste, social status, or financial prowess.

Sudesh rarely wore make-up or entertained fancy hairdos. She was more of a plain Jane and get up and go- kind of girl. Yet today, as she stared back at her reflection in the mirror, she couldn't help but feel drawn in, as if by her vanity itself, as she caught a glimpse of something within her reflection, she'd not taken stock of before. Like the fact that even without any make-up, fancy hairdos, or trendy and expensive clothes, there was still something yielding about her. An effortless attraction within the symmetry of her face. The peek arch of her prominent brow. The blush on her high cheekbone. The moonlit sparkle, deep inside her dark-set eyes. That shadowy effect from her naturally long lashes. That sharp edge of her jawline, on top of her alluring long neck. That tiny dip inside her fair chin. Even the cupid's bow, crowning her pink lips, stood out today. Alongside the cascades of her jet black hair, almost framing her face like a portrait of art, it was the first time she could see what others had seen. The very first time, she believed their words and realised that, yes, indeed, she was quite pretty after all.

TANGLES

"Yesterday I was clever, so I wanted to change the world.
Today I am wise, so I am changing myself" Rumi

The clock in the hallway ticked ever closer to 6 pm. It was almost time! Snapping herself out of her indulgent gaze, she instructed herself-

Ok! You must confront him about the letter today! Who does he think he is? Just one kiss, and what?... That's it!... Am I now his- to freely say he loves me? Just like that? I bet he's just playing games! I bet he doesn't even mean it! He's just trying to make a fool of me- for fun! He thinks he's so funny! Well, I will show him! One word, just one little word to my brother, and that- will wipe that stupid smile off his stupid face!

She tried to stay angry. She wanted to hate him for the sake of courage. In her desperate plea to prepare for this fight ahead, she'd have to remain strong. It had gone too far! He'd gone too far! She had to end this battle of wills between them, which she now realised, had started that very day- when she'd failed her exam and when he had come to the house to visit Raj and had suddenly, so very gallantly refused- to eat his food; until she did! *Yes! That was the day it all started!* She realised. *That was the first time; she'd stupidly given in to him, let him make a fool of her, and, most importantly, get his way! And that was the moment that sealed her fate!*

Continuing to comb her long hair gently at first, she clocked the time and proceeded with urgency. In haste, she formed a stubborn tangle in her hair, tightly trapped inside the comb. Trying to ease it out, she carefully unravelled; strand after strand; to free the comb. But it wouldn't budge. Instead, it seemed to be entangling even more. Becoming increasingly impatient, she plucked a whole chunk of hair from her head as a sudden pain stung her scalp. She wanted to scream out and cry, but she didn't. She withstood the pain through her gritted teeth and defiantly continued yanking away at the comb. She was determined to free it and make her lesson on time, with her hair fully done! She had no intention of appearing sloppy. Not least, in front of him! She realised it was high time that she stepped up and behaved maturely. Someone had to! Someone had to be sensible and wise about things and keep stock of what was best- for them both. He- clearly couldn't! Besides, she was determined that nothing and no one would ruin her chances for success, not even him!

Finally, she'd freed the comb and, with it, a whole chunk of her hair! Then, flippantly flipping it aside, she quickly ran out of her house and straight on towards his- with each step, ever stronger and ever more determined than the one before.

SUCKER PUNCH

Persistently banging on Inder's front door; until her knuckles hurt; her adrenaline pumped through her veins, straight through into the hard thuds of her fist. To her surprise, he promptly opened it as if he was already there, waiting on the other side. With her fist mid-air, she looked at him, slightly taken aback. He looked at her, somewhat dumbfounded, with a curious intrigue in his ever-smiling eyes. Predictably, he tried to break the ice with humour, suddenly ducking as if in defence of an incoming sucker punch! Promptly lowering her arm and feeling slightly foolish while wishing she'd, in fact, punched his smug face! - She looked at him defiantly and unimpressed, her glaring eyeballs on him, like a standoff with a grizzly bear and as if that alone might scare him away! But she quickly realised; it would take more than a mean stare for him to falter! Sheepishly grinning at her before bowing down in an exaggerated welcome, he annoyed her even more by reminding her of his patronising sister Hema and her antics! Now more irritated, she swished past him like a gust of wind and marched down the hallway toward his study room. His nonchalant expression pierced into her staunch back as his eyes followed her, and she fought for her equanimity with every fibre of being. Quashing her sudden urge to kick his perfectly polished shoes out of her way, she entered the study room. He followed behind her as the little hairs on her neck erected up towards him.

ELEPHANT

"But he, that dares not grasp the thorn should never crave the rose" Anne Bronte

They both sat and were instantly aware of the giant elephant; that silently sat in the room with them. The two hours; passed by slowly! All the time, both remained poker-faced and focused on their tasks. Both; trying to look at *anything* but one another and trying to think about *anything* but each other! Still, in certain minuscule moments; they'd both fall witness to that second's awkwardness and the inescapable presence of that *giant elephant in the room!* Who still stubbornly sat in wait as if looking upon them both as silly fools. Momentarily catching one another's gaze from the corner of their eyes, they fought for calm composures within their quietly quivering bodies. On the slightest of occasions, something would nonetheless jar. Like an odd note, playing out of tune, or a strange phrase- misplaced within stilted conversations and words dropped out of their incoherent sentences. Feelings mixed up and scattered like haphazard droplets of rain upon a windowpane- blurring any clear vision and each sentence spoken through pierced lips, caught inside strange stutters and mumbles under their breath. Their words; were about something and nothing at all. Both, impaired like fumbling drunken fools; suffering from moments of time lapses, seconds of memory loss, and strange amnesia; seemed as if caught inside a hazy snowfall. The atmosphere was so heavy, holding them hostage inside all their unsaid words and all the unacceptable, inescapable truths hanging between them like barbed wire. Each one, unexpectedly flinching, within that all too familiar anticipation of *something*; inside each hesitation, harboured with expectation...

As the end of the lesson drew near, she swiftly got up and gathered her belongings before taking a long deep breath and, feeling suddenly parched, grabbed the glass of cold lemonade. Gulping it down- whole, she turned to face him, barely able to ignore that sudden brain-freeze within. Their eyes locked as her legs weakened beneath her, and she held the edge of the desk to stabilise herself from collapse. It took every ounce of strength and courage to speak as he looked at her, through her, and almost as if- inside her. His slightly alarmed face hid behind his reticence and secretly smug smile, waiting for her to speak...

"Listen!" She'd started strong and a tad louder than anticipated! "Why... Why did you write that letter?" she then whispered loudly.

He looked at her blankly, almost slightly confused, and for a split second, she was mortified by the prospect- *that she may have got it all wrong! That maybe, she'd made a grave error of judgment? Maybe, just maybe, that note was not for her! Perhaps, it was not even from him!?*

"Huh? What letter?" He asked, so cool as a cucumber, while clearing his desk, picking the single biscuit, and holding it out towards him with a slight smirk.

She shook her head and right then, she knew it! - instantly and instinctively, she knew! He promptly ate the biscuit himself- looking straight at her, almost seductively and fleetingly reminding her of that day- when she, too, was obliged to eat before him and had chewed her food- so rudely into his face! But this time, her eyes felt drawn in close... too close- to his munching lips! Still, she could tell; he was trying too hard- acting too cool! And *that* was a dead giveaway!

"You know what bloody letter! Don't try to make a fool of me! She asserted, as her temperature rose with how incorrigible he could be! "What if I show it to my brother?" she raised her eyebrows and the stakes.

"What indeed..." he goaded her "but... if there is no signature, how can you prove it was from me?" He asked, sly as a snake, before pushing his chin close to hers in an almost childish stand-off.

For a split millisecond, they both fought a sudden desire to laugh out loud! Maybe even kiss!... his lips, her lips... She shrugged it off! *Back to the point! That's it! I've got you!* She felt victorious with adrenaline.

"Oh! So, then, you must know what letter? Otherwise, how could you possibly know; that there's no signature? Hmmm?" *Yes! Yes! She had him! A-star for me!*

She smiled childishly, mirroring his smugness, like a cat who'd got the cream! *Haha! Not so clever, after all, are you?* She thought, watching his façade crumbling before her, with no come back- for once! Instead, he went on to nod his head, almost as if he was somehow impressed by his little prodigy and her clever detective work! She waited for his response. But it never came. Unable to think of what else to say or do, she took a long, drawn-out breath and, before taking her leave, momentarily caught a glimpse of his widening smirk behind her.

She hated how he always confused her heart and mind.

BACK TO BUSINESS

> *"Your past does not equal your future"* Tony Robbins

Days turned into weeks, and her butterflies started to settle, just as Inder became happily preoccupied with so many other things in his life and seemingly now unbothered with entertaining his previous confessions of love! Unsure whether he'd had a change of heart or if she'd sufficiently scared him off- while feeling victorious, she also felt irritated by how easily he'd given up. He'd proved- only that he didn't mean anything he'd said or done. Admittedly, a small part of her couldn't help but wonder about those - *What ifs...?* But she was at least relieved that matters weren't being further complicated. Remaining adamant, she would not let anything jeopardize her study success, especially not something which now seemed so inconsequential and, most likely, just a silly, insignificant blip of nonsense by Inder! That searing love story, which Santosh had convinced herself of and seemingly created more so in her mind; still had her bombarding Sudesh with questions about *what had happened* every time she saw her after tuition, and Sudesh would always answer, much the same; 'Nothing!' Feeling partly relieved and partly disappointed, she tried her best to forget about it. If nothing else, then just for the sake of her sanity!

As time passed, she'd convinced herself that the whole episode; was simply part of a sick joke and windup and, as incredulous as it may seem, most likely just part of Inder's nonsensical sense of humour! After all, she reasoned; *If his feelings and words had been genuine and sincere, he'd surely, have put up a bigger fight for her. Surely, he'd not have given up at the very first hurdle? Surely, she was worth more than that?* Alas, nothing ventured- nothing gained!

STATUS QUO

Inder's family situation was far from being; a happy one! With two overbearing sisters and a formidable mother, the males in the house appeared as if spiritually emasculated! Routinely treated as inferior beings, it was contrary to how things were in Sudesh's and, indeed, in most other Indian households. Although Sudesh resented inequality, especially against females, she nonetheless sympathised with Inder. Having witnessed first-hand; his unusual second-class status at home and how often his father unnecessarily pandered to the female's demands. Simple choices around- what could be eaten and drunk and when; were strictly controlled by the females; from their otherwise- out-of-bounds kitchen. Even the most basic task of making an impromptu cup of tea was frowned upon; if a female wasn't present, to oblige! Being such an independent and self-sufficient, modern-day man, Inder had always preferred doing things for himself, how and when he liked. He resented having to rely on others and having to answer to anyone. Consequently, he'd often appear anxious and stressed when at home. With the palpable tension, always lingering in the air, and if they weren't arguing over something trivial- like who can make a cup of tea? Instead, the deadly silence hung like a heavy cloud of vapourised stench between them, harbouring all their built-up resentments and simply waiting for an almighty downpour!

10

FALLING

"Life appears to me too short to be spent in nursing animosity or registering wrongs" - 'Jane Eyre' Charlotte Bronte

HOMEMADE SOAP

When Sudesh realised Inder's family made their own homemade soap, it was as if she'd finally solved a long-standing puzzle inside her head. *Finally, it all made sense! - Why his house consistently smelt like talcum powder? Why empty bottles and containers littered the place, and why was it always so annoyingly hot there?*

Although making soap to sell was illegal, Inder's family primarily made it for their own consumption, and luckily, their sympathetic neighbours turned a blind eye. Relatively inexpensive to produce, soap was still rather dangerous and time-consuming to make, with the monthly task designated to Inder and his brother

One Saturday afternoon, while home alone and keen to get a head start, Inder was painstakingly carrying his fifth bucket full of hot soapy mixture; when he decided it was high time, he took a break and quenched his thirst. But, unfortunately, no sooner had he decided; that he suddenly lost his footing and spilled the entire contents of piping hot soapy mixture all over the alleyway floors, as well as himself! The loud thud of his fall and the sound of the bucket ricocheting down the alleyway; were quickly followed by the sound of his screeches from having burnt his leg! Fortunately, Sudesh was home and tending to her garden, and upon recognising Inder's voice- calling for help; she stopped dead in her tracks and immediately bolted out of her house, straight towards his. Frantically following the sounds of his cries, she found Inder helplessly lying in the alleyway, with the steaming hot liquid still vaporising off the floor and his badly scolded leg! Struggling to lift him, she cried out for her mother, who also appeared shortly after hearing the commotion and helped raise Inder, into the house, before calling for an ambulance.

At that moment, whilst instantly in floods of tears and rushing about almost hysterically, Sudesh couldn't help but feel overwhelming concern for him and his well-being. Her obvious distress from seeing him in pain caused such a strong visceral reaction that it could not be contained or hidden and, clearly, seemed disproportionate, with the fact that Inder was merely her brother's friend! And, it had not escaped her mother's attention either! Luckily, her mother was too preoccupied with helping Inder and distracted enough to forgo challenging or confronting her daughter about her overtly emotional reaction right then.

In the following weeks, Sudesh attended the GP surgery for medication collections, coincidentally while Inder was being treated for his burns and having his wounds redressed. Upon hearing him crying out in pain from the adjacent nurse's room, she'd continually feel an overwhelming urge to go to his aid. But knowing she couldn't, she instead started to pray. It was the only thing she could do. Henceforth, she found herself praying day and night, especially for Inder, and as the days passed, she sensed a certain shifting inside of herself. Like a steady unveiling of the truth, she had realised that her initial worry and sympathy for Inder; was sure enough turning into something far more profound, and it was the very thing; she'd feared feeling the most...

Love!

TYPHOID

A few weeks after Inder's recovery, Sudesh herself had fallen ill. Hit with a severe case of typhoid! Left fully isolated, within a separate room for two weeks and in this entirely bedridden state, she'd at least managed to escape her father's endless chores and sporadic episodes of rage, and although she felt desperately unwell, it was a relief to be free of the family's ongoing dramas too! With all her meals delivered to her bedroom door and in a timely fashion- if it wasn't for her terrible body aches and roaring loud cough, she could almost be fooled into thinking; she was on her own little holiday!

SWEET HOPE

"Sometimes the smallest things take the most room in your heart" Winnie the pooh

With just one day remaining; of her fourteen-day isolation period, the novelty of having her personal space and me time; was fast wearing off! Besieged with restless boredom and increasing claustrophobia, she lay in bed for hours with nothing for company but her niggling, intrusive and conflicting thoughts. Spinning inside her unstimulated mind, veering ever closer to the brink of insanity, along with her high fever-inducing further delirium, she felt as if the walls themselves were caving in on her! And one reoccurring image played at the forefront of her mind all the while... that *first-ever kiss!* And one single name echoed inside her head, every waking moment... *Inder!* Finally, like a tiny droplet of water quenching a marooned traveller's lips, she heard a new voice calling her from the other side of her bedroom door. After realising it wasn't in her head, and someone had, at last, been permitted to visit her- albeit from a safe distance, she was further delighted when she realised it was her dear friend, Santosh! Who'd bought her a very special message from a very secret admirer!

"Sudesssssssh! Heeee saaaaaid...!" Santosh hissed like an alley cat behind the door as Sudesh forcefully crawled closer and pushed her ear against the wooden door, desperately trying to comprehend her hushed whispers.

"Whaaaaat? Whooooo said what? Speak up! I can't even hear you!" Sudesh desperately cried.

"I can't! Dammit! I said- heeeee said- *heeeee really missesss you! Nobody to drink his lem-on-ade and eat his cheeeeap biscuits!*"

Santosh giggled wildly, "Seeeee! Told you, didn't I- that he is serioooous? Get better quick-leeeee! Inder is waiting for yooou! Shit! Someone's coming! I must go!" and with her, her hisses quickly trailed away too.

What bittersweet words- *Inder is waiting!* She thought as the words continued reverberating in her mind; long after, her friend had gone. Her words were like snowflakes falling on an icy floor; making her instantaneously feel better! Like a switch suddenly turned on, like a bolt of lightning had shot through her veins, recharging her very being. With her mind and body re-energised and reawakened in excitement, everything, everywhere, felt reignited again! That message was the perfect antidote to her sickness, the most excellent medicine, producing the most incredible feeling of...*hope!* Without which, there seemed to be no point or reason for anything, and she had decided that very afternoon- *she would sneak herself out with her little sister Kiran and join her, for an impromptu shopping trip, to the local bazaar! And just in time for Diwali, she would buy herself, the brightest, most beautiful- rainbow-coloured Parandi, she could find and wear it in sweet celebration; of this sweet, sweet hope! It would be like a colourful confetti sky appearing after a dark storm!* Having secretly scrimped and saved a few rupees, she'd just enough to buy one, and spurred on by her unquestionable desire, she got herself ready. Once the coast was clear, and she heard Kiran- at the front door, she quickly ran out and sneaked up next to her!

"Surpriiiiiiiiiiiiiiise!" She squealed, appearing like an apparition by Kiran's side and making her almost jump out of her skin!

"Whaaaat!? Are you crazy? You shouldn't be out! There is still *one day* left before...!" Kiran vainly pleaded in shock.

"Shuuush! It is ok! Just trust me! One day- it doesn't make any difference! And look! Look! I am all better now! Seeeeeee!" Sudesh twirled around, full of bubbles.

Giggling at the front door like two naughty schoolgirls, they hastily left, with Sudesh's head bowed down and fully covered beneath her chunni scarf, as she sneaked in a quick eyeful of Inder's house, noting- it was still there, just the same. But sadly, with no sight of him! Noticing Sudesh looking up from under her shroud, Kiran quickly yanked Sudesh's head back down again and fully covered it while huffing and puffing in shock!

"Keep bloody down! - Stupid idiot!" she shouted, still reeling from what she'd let herself get talked into!

Sudesh giggled away under her chunni scarf, as they headed ever faster towards the busy bazaar, both quietly praying;

"Please, God! Please don't let anyone catch us out together!"

RELAPSE

> *"Sometimes things fall apart, so better things can fall together"* Marilyn Monroe

The impromptu shopping trip proved a grave mistake! On her return home, overcome with weakness and unable to lift her arms, she'd almost collapsed to the floor- had her mother not hurtled forward- just in time to save her!

"Sudeeeeeesh!" she cried out, "Offo! Yahaan kya kar rahe hai? Hey Bhaghvaan! *(What are you doing here? Oh God!)*"

Shocked; to see Sudesh, not only out of isolation- a day early but also fully dressed and having been out shopping- her mother was stunned! But after feeling Sudesh's burning hot forehead, she decided to save a proper telling-off for later and promptly called the emergency doctor instead. After examining her, the doctor concurred- her Typhoid had relapsed due to her carelessness. Sternly reprimanding her, he marched her back to her room to isolate an additional fourteen days before brazenly handing her poor mother another hefty medical bill and a long prescription list.

When Sudesh's father got heed, he was fuming and had her condition not been so precarious and contagious- he'd likely have beaten her half to death! Instead, as usual, her poor mother suffered the brunt of it, taking full blame for '...not sufficiently having watched her rotten spoilt kids!'

Later that evening, after callously ripping Sudesh's new rainbow-coloured Parandi to shreds, her father ordered the entire family- 'to keep away from her!' and even forbade them from feeding her anything!

As she lay in her bed, shivering and feeling desperately hungry, she could still hear her father's rage reverberating through the walls long into the night!

"Ye jie ya mare mujhe koee phark nahin padata! Koee bhee use khaane ya peene ke lie kuchh nahin dega, jab tak ki main kaho! *(If she lives or dies, I do not care! No one will give her anything to eat or drink until I say!)*."

Her mother spent the next few days carefully trying to orchestrate clever ways to feed her daughter secretly. Yet still, Sudesh's Typhoid went from bad to worse over the next few days. Her condition deteriorated so much that she couldn't keep food or liquid down, in any case! Slowly wasting away before their very eyes and in her bedridden state, she couldn't help but wonder whether-

...all the recent suffering- was simply part of God's cardinal punishment- for her and Inder's immoral, unholy thoughts and desires? And maybe, they were being punished for their forbidden love- before marriage?

A firm believer in fate and karma, she had become increasingly convinced that Inder's sudden accident and her sudden life-threatening Typhoid; were not mere coincidences but some karmic payback and penance.

Before long, her family was confronted with the fact that Sudesh; was not getting any better. It seemed that no matter what medicine they tried, nothing worked, and her inability to eat and drink further weakened her body- day by day and made it even harder for her to fight this cruel illness. She'd now lost so much weight; she was barely recognisable and merely skin and bones! At her weakest, she needed assistance with everything, from toileting to lifting herself in and out of bed. Even changing positions in bed; to avoid bed sores; required others to help. A few days on, the doctor made his final visit before planning to hospitalise Sudesh into palliative care.

"If this tablet doesn't work, then there's nothing else left to do!" He soberly warned, holding out a panacea in the form of a single little yellow pill! "... I'm afraid her condition has become *very* serious now and life-threatening! You must all prepare for the worse!"

Understandably, the news brought everyone great distress; for most of them, it was the fear of losing Sudesh; but for their father; it seemed the concern was more about how much her treatment and prolonged stay in the hospital before she *finally died-* might cost!

"Usaka ilaaj sambhav nahin hai! Use marane do! Vah marane laayak hai! Sab usakee galatee hai! *(Her treatment is unaffordable! Let her die! She deserves to die! It's all her own fault!)*." he ranted.

As Sudesh nervously took the pill, her lamenting mother prayed, through streams of tears- "Hey Bhagavaan, meree betee ko bachao! *(Oh God, save my daughter!)*"

Most unexpectedly, Sudesh managed to keep the little yellow pill down, and within an hour of taking it, she'd finally started to show some promising signs of improvement. With her temperature gradually stabilising, they were finally able to get her to keep down tiny drops of liquid again, and soon, this was followed by bits of puréed foods. Before, she was finally back onto solids again. With each passing day, her body and mind regained their former strength, and with it, she also started to challenge her morbid and negative thoughts, gradually replacing them with more positive and hopeful ones. Her desire to live and to pick up where she'd left off in life and with Inder; was quickly followed by a single yearning; to again see his face... *his beautiful face* once again. She'd sure kept him waiting long enough!

SHIMLA

An accomplished cricket player, Inder was also an exceptionally skilled bowler. A member of the popular- 'All India Radio Cricket Team,' he had a match in the beautiful and remote hill station area of Shimla and would be away for a further two weeks, on top of the three months they'd already spent apart! When asked- if she'd like to squeeze in an extra math session just before his trip, needless to say, she couldn't help but jump at the chance!

11

LEMONADE

"The pain of parting is nothing, to the joy of meeting again" Charles Dickens 'A Tale of Two Cities'

BISCUITS

She checked her reflection in the mirror one last time before racing out of her front door and landing herself- 6 pm sharp at his front door. Even the pouring rain; could not halter her speed. His immediate smile filled her with warmth; this time, her beaming smile back at him; was impossible to deny. He looked so handsome; he *was* so handsome, more handsome than she'd ever remembered him being. And this time, the sight of his shiny polished shoes, placed neatly outside his study door, did not irritate her in the slightest, and it seemed as if everything was being experienced for the first time again as if she was looking through a new set of eyes, filled with a *new hope*. Skewing her perspective upon an axel, all that was once irritating was strangely warm and familiar instead. Now, the warmth inside his house felt comforting and cosy. And that clean, fresh soapy smell was refreshing, alongside the rich sandalwood scent permeating off his slightly exposed upper chest. In retrospect, his house wasn't messy after all, and that previously cramped study room; now felt more like a cradling snug. Shyly awkward at first, they'd soon settled into some polite conversation, albeit skating around their health and the weather!

"How are you- feeling now?" He asked gently, his concern etched into his frown lines.

"Oh... better, thank you... and your leg- it is better?" she earnestly enquired.

"Very good now- just a little bit scarring- but at least the pain is less! Thank God!" He grimaced.

"Yes, thank God" she said.

"Oh ho! I must thank you- *you and your mother*. Don't know what would I have done- if you all were not home," he looked almost taken with emotion.

"It was nothing, nothing..." she replied flippantly. "I'm happy- it was not even worse! Least your *one* other leg is still ok!" she giggled nervously. "But I think... it is too dangerous...?"

An awkward silence took hold.

"Huh?... dangerous?" he was slightly nervous.

"Yes... too dangerous..." she shook her head and sighed. Then noticing his confusion- "...I mean... all this... making soap... at home... is too dangerous" she said softly.

"Oh! Soap! Yes! Hmmm... but, don't you think... some danger is worth it?" he asked knowingly, smirking at her. She looked away as another awkward silence took hold, "Looks like- rain has stopped" he tried changing the subject, looking thoughtfully out of the window, with his head lifted towards the rays of sunlight.

She watched on, mesmerised by his beautiful face, as the sun-lit stardust seemed to orbit him and he looked like her very own Adonis reincarnated; stood before her in his mortal form, and she- like his very own Goddess Aphrodite, was as if folly-fallen at his feet. Then, sensing her stare, he snapped out of his thoughts and swiftly returned to her side as she looked away again, catching another alluring waft of his sweet scent brushing past her nostrils. Soon enough, returning to the familiar confines of their math books, they sat side by side like old friends, meeting after a short hiatus. Yet even still, a charge was in the air, alongside an undeniable and deepening yearning, inside the flutters of their pelvises! And whenever his warm breath brushed past her cheek, she'd feel a slight tremble inside. At times, both quietly quivered within their own mini earthquakes and held onto the edges of the shifting planes, hoping to survive the mini tremors alongside any seismic quakes! As tuition ended, he handed her the glass of cold lemonade.

"Sorry... the ice has melted... I know you always feel hot here" he looked apologetic.

"It's ok. It's not that hot today. Besides, too much ice isn't good for my throat," she politely replied, taking the glass, as an electric shock passed from his little finger to hers.

She drank the lemonade in one full swig! As Inder gently laughed, before holding out the small plate with, this time, two biscuits placed upon it.

"Two biscuits?" she inquired, slightly surprised, "...you trying to make me fat, or were they on extra cheap offer?" she playfully teased him.

"You need to keep your strength up. You have lost much weight..." He studied her figure with slight alarm, making her instantly self-conscious.

"We both need our strength..." she coiled in with shyness, "Ok- one for you and one for me?" she smiled, taking just one biscuit.

He smiled back at her and, then took the other biscuit. Walking towards the front door, both munching on their biscuits, they tried to think of what else they could say. Before he opened the front door and, somewhat surprisingly, asked her-

"So, what Birthday gift would you like from Shimla? 22nd, isn't it?"

"Huh? Gift?" she was caught off guard and impressed he'd remembered her birthday!

"Umm...umm..." Although, given time, she'd likely have thought of many cool gifts she could've asked him to bring from the popular tourist destination of Shimla! - instead she said- "Just win and come back"

Shyly walking away, with his stare tickling the hairs on her neck, she wondered- *if he, too, felt that flutter in his pelvis, or that strong tug, from the very centre of his chest, like that of a magnet, pulling them back together again?*

CLOCK

The two weeks felt like forever! She'd missed him dearly. Those couple of hours of tuition each week had long since been the very highlight of her entire week and what she most looked forward to. In those two hours- with him, she felt more alive, with every cell in her body, than she ever had. She checked the date on her wall calendar meticulously every day. Using her marker pen, she'd tick off each day, counting down ever closer to the day of his return. Closer and closer to that magnetic pull- which got stronger and stronger as she got ever closer to that date and closer to him and his face... *his beautiful face. Soon...! Soon...!* she kept reassuring herself.

Finally, the day had come! January 22nd- also her 17th birthday! Looking out of the front room window, over and over, she tried to catch sight of his return at the house opposite. But she'd either missed him or, worse still, he'd not returned! But luckily, with the next session booked for the next day, she held tightly onto the hope; that he'd be there to greet her. It was the longest night on record! When dawn broke, she obsessively started watching her clock, checking it- hour upon hour, counting down every hour until her plight would be over! *Please let it be 5.55 pm!* She urged the clock, imagining her feet taking her to him, already imagining his beautiful smile at the front door and her immediate collapse into his arms. She took extra care readying herself. Making everything perfect; a whole two hours before! But her doubts and fears probed inside, with a distant nagging voice, and she also couldn't help but wonder- *if Inder had had fun in Shimla, fun without her? If his team had won the match and celebrated with alcohol and partied the nights away with all those beautiful and exotic, Hill-Station girls?* She could imagine those girls, specially hired for their beauty and allure and specially called upon to entertain and entice the new male guests and wealthy tourists and encourage them to spend more money! She tried to distract her racing thoughts by again studying her clock keenly. Time- her fickle enemy, was so annoyingly slow! She picked it up and shook it, wondering; *if it was faulty, had slowed down, or stopped. Why does each second and minute feel so frustratingly slow today? Hurry, time... hurry!* She pleaded, like a girl gone mad, maddened by love!

6 pm sharp; she stood at his front door, cradling her book bag to her chest and excitedly knocking. Fighting her desperate urge to fall into his arms, as soon as she saw him, open that door! But just her luck, a blank-faced Hema opened the door instead! - instantly deflating every ounce of her excitement, by her stinging sour face!

"She's here again!" Hema sternly declared; before abruptly walking away.

Sudesh took a long deep breath to steady her nerves before walking in. That first sign he was home was always his perfectly polished, perfectly placed shoes at his study room door. Then, finally him...!

There you are...! she thought.

There you are...! He thought.

Their eyes locked in momentarily. Both hearts skipped a beat; both held their breaths... until a loud thudding sound came crashing through from the kitchen! *Hema! Of course!* Both instantly snapped out of their wanton stare as he- resumed his role as her designated teacher, and she- resumed hers; as his designated student once again! *Bloody, bloody Hema!* They both thought at once!

MISSING BISCUIT

"Love makes fools of all of us"? William Thackery

Like the ice in her lemonade awaiting her thirsty lips, the excitement, which had been building up inside her for two whole weeks, too- had dissipated and melted away. And then, when she noticed *no biscuit* beside her lemonade glass, she was instantly perplexed. Although she'd hardly ever eaten it, its absence stung her like salt upon an open wound today. She opened her math book, fighting a compelling urge to ask him; *Not* how his trip was. *Not* if he'd won the match? *Not* even if he'd missed her? But something else, which now seemed so strangely pertinent today- 'Where is my *biscuit?*' She'd unknowingly become a creature of habit, comfortable in patterns and familiarity, and now, this damn missing biscuit; had her questioning so many other things! She wondered *if their separation had changed something, maybe everything? If perhaps, alongside this absent biscuit, his affections for her were now absent too?* But she decided to keep quiet, feeling too coy to probe him and seeing him acting; so strangely formal- having forgotten even to wish her for her Birthday! As the lesson came to an end, he lifted the glass of lemonade out toward her;

"Not thirsty today?" he smirked, seeming almost sarcastic.

Feeling instantly irritated, she glared at him, still fighting her urge to ask him about her missing biscuit. Instead, she abruptly snatched the glass from his hand and gulped the lemonade down in one hit. The ice shocked her into an instant brain freeze! Yet, refusing to let him see her in pain, she kept her face frozen as the shooting pain travelled from her head to her face and then onto her throat, turning everything numb! Still, she kept her composure and her eyes fixed on him. Once again, she was caught trying to prove a point. Once again, they'd found themselves in the clutches of a familiar stand-off. That old battle of wills, rearing up with its ugly head, and yet again, *the point* of it all gone amiss! Surprised and intrigued, he looked at her as if wondering; *...what a strange creature she was?* But as his smirk crept back onto his face, she felt annoyed again and abruptly slammed the empty glass onto his desk. The sudden noise; made them both slightly flinch; before she hastily grabbed her belongings and bolted out the door. His eyes, following her leave, and the magnets pull even stronger!

She hated how he always confused her heart and mind!

KEYRING

On arriving home and while emptying her book bag, a strange object she didn't recognise; fell out. An unusually plain black keyring, which she'd never seen before. *Whose keyring is this?* She wondered, *maybe, it belonged to someone from Inder's house? Perhaps, she'd accidentally picked it; while grabbing her things in haste? Oh no! I hope it's not bloody- Hema's!* She fretted as she sat on the edge of her bed and wondered whether to take it back. But just then, another thought occurred to her... *maybe, Inder had purposefully put it there? Perhaps, this was her long-anticipated gift- from Shimla? But it just didn't make sense! For today, he'd not even bothered to offer her a single stale biscuit or even wish her Happy Birthday! So why would he have bothered giving her this strange gift?* Utterly unimpressed, she seriously questioned his taste and stingy nature! And yet still, she couldn't help but wonder- *if he was up to his old tricks? If he'd purposefully given her this rather insignificant gift- to tease her for a joke? She certainly wouldn't put it past him!*

Annoyed by his silly humour, she continued to rotate the keyring in her hands. Before suddenly noticing a little instruction label stuck to its back, reading-

'Blow on my surface, and my magic message shall appear!'

Instantly intrigued, she gently blew on the keyring's surface, and to her utter surprise and delight- three rather unexpected words; suddenly appeared!... *'I LOVE YOU!'*

Almost balled over in surprise and instantly overjoyed, she felt a great sense of excitement and relief! *How wrong she had been about Inder and his taste! Indeed, this was one of the most delightful, novel, and romantic gifts she'd ever seen! And those were the very best three words ever written or said!* As the words slowly appeared and disappeared- as if by magic, with each breath, she continued to blow upon the keyring surface- again and again. With her faith finally restored, and her hope finally relit, she bought the keyring to her lips and kissed it. Wishing, instead of the keyring, she was kissing his *lips!*

SECRET ADMIRER

They were waiting for their Home Economics teacher to arrive at class alongside their peers. Suddenly remembering; she'd not yet shown Santosh her lovely gift, Sudesh discreetly took her keyring out from her bag. Excitedly holding it up to Santosh, she exclaimed with zeal;

"Look! Look what Inder gave me! My birthday gift from *Shimla!*"

As expected, Santosh, too, looked utterly unimpressed, just like Sudesh; by the plain blank keyring and wondered- 'why her friend was so excited over such a pitiful gift?'

"What is this? Is this what he got you?" Santosh asked, surprised by Inder's lack of imagination and poor gift taste!

"No, wait! Wait!" Sudesh insisted as she pulled Santosh closer; "Just blow on it; then you'll see what happens!"

Santosh rolled her eyes impatiently and then, raising her eyebrows with cynicism, reluctantly obliged. Just before she'd given up and looked away, she caught sight of the three anticipated words, appearing as if by magic! Gasping out aloud, she was immediately enchanted; as she held the keyring up towards the sunlight and excitedly blew on it again and again. Both girls giggled wildly, as they watched the words appear and disappear with delight. Just then, an annoyingly curious fellow student; had suddenly lunged forward and, without hesitation, snatched the keyring and run away!

"Oi! Oi! Give it back, hey!" Santosh gave chase across the classroom as hysteria prevailed!

But the girl was too quick-footed, and now a small crowd had gathered around, blocking Santosh and Sudesh out; as they all excitedly passed the keyring around. Blowing on the keyring, one after the next, and falling over themselves in excited laughter before screeching out, over and over again!

"Oooooh… Ooooh... I looooooove yoooooou! I love you! I love you!"

Finally, Sudesh managed to retrieve her keyring; just as their teacher walked into class to resume the lesson and the usually long and tedious Home Economics class had been filled with excitement and gossip today! Leaving all the curious and envious students wondering- 'Who Sudesh's secret admirer was? And who it was, that had declared their love to her- with such a cool and novel gift?'... the likes of which no one had ever seen before!

FINDERS KEEPERS

The next session reverted to a routine and formal feel. It was becoming harder to rely on consistency between them concerning Inder's mood and how he made her feel around him. Each time, it felt like a gamble- how friendly or unfriendly, how formal or informal, and how calm or annoying he might be! Constantly on tenter-hooks, she walked into the study room each time, wondering- which version of him; she'd be getting today. With the uncertainty, playing havoc on her nerves and that delicate balance of their relationship, constantly bouncing between the blurred lines- of a student and tutor, neighbour and family friend, and now, metamorphosed into something divergent between all of that and the man... she now loved! It became mind-bending and precarious to manage. Often, it was only upon his que; that she could adapt her behaviour and navigate their time spent. With the ball, always in his court, as the senior person in control—the one in that position of power and holding the highest cards and most significant stake. Wrought with trepidation, they constantly walked upon a tightrope- stretched out between them, to the point of either snapping or being pulled out too far to return. But today, as she started packing her belongings; she'd finally mustered her courage. She'd decided to confront him about the keyring and wondered *why he couldn't just be straight and honest with her and hand her a gift like a normal person. Why he played all these silly games and kept her always; second guessing everything?* She was sick of all the unclear declarations, half-said and half held within!

"Why did you give me that keyring?" She frankly asked him as he stopped what he was doing and looked taken aback.

"Oh... So, you liked it?" he smirked.

"Ummm... maybe! ... Maybe not!" She stubbornly replied, half teasing him.

"Oh!... Ok then! If you don't like it- give it back! Maybe, I will give it to someone- who does!" He teased her back; before abruptly picking up the glass of lemonade and drinking it and then devouring the single biscuit too! He was incorrigible! Now even more irritated than before, having looked forward to enjoying her cold lemonade and little biscuit, she snapped her math book shut and quickly took her leave, with that magnetising pull, ever harder to escape!

She hated how he confused her heart and mind!

SWEET SURRENDER

The following session, there were two glasses of ice-cold lemonade and two biscuits placed upon his desk. At the end of tuition, she sensed him close behind her... too close! So close; So close, that the hairs on the back of her neck lifted and released from his inhale and exhale. So close that the magnets in their chests; were almost about to snap! Then, as she turned to face him, he leaned in even closer. Before his lips were tightly on hers and the world melted away. This time... she did not resist!

12

LOVER'S DREAM

*"I knew from the beginning of time that I was
yours and you were mine"*

EXTRA STUDY

Over the next few weeks, Sudesh and Inder met for tuition a few more times- than usual. On the assumption that she'd already missed core study time due to their bouts of ill health and knowing that her exam was impending, they'd effectively pulled the wool over everyone's eyes, although in truth, they spent most of their supposed study time; less on studying their math's books and more on studying- one another! He'd now pick her up from around the corner of their homes and take her on his scooter; to ride the thermals of their lover's dream. With Santosh being the only person privy to this secret rendezvous and acting as a willing accomplice and occasionally as a trusted alibi!

The Math's retake exam; was just days away, and with all her mock tests, having come back with promisingly high marks, both teacher and student were quietly confident and optimistic; that this time around, she'd pass! However, what truly worried them both, was not; what Sudesh's pass mark would or would not be or whether she'd pass or fail. But- *how on earth would they continue to see one another- once the exam was over? What possible excuse or legitimate reason- they'd have to spend any time together alone once tuition was over?* With the harsh reality dawning upon them like a sledgehammer, they both realised that even using Santosh as an excuse; wouldn't prove enough to satiate their famished desires!

SCORED

"You have to know what sparks, that light in you, so that you, in your own way, can illuminate the world" Oprah Winfrey

When the day of Sudesh's Math exam arrived, she could barely believe her luck! Almost every question on her paper; seemed identical to the mock paper Inder had last set her! Having scored 98% previously, she managed to whiz her way through the paper in almost half the allocated time, practically skipping her way out of the exam hall in the safe knowledge; she'd finally nailed it!

Weeks on, as her results day arrived, she woke early, eagerly awaiting the postman's arrival. Just like before, no sooner had he knocked on the front door that she'd already run straight up to him and hastily snatched the newspaper out of his hands! Once again, leaving her poor mum to face the embarrassment of her daughter's abrupt rudeness! With the building anticipation making her hands clammy, the paper's fresh ink had already transferred black ink blotches upon her fair hands as she tightly gripped it and scanned her eagle eyes in that familiar search of her roll number. Stumbling upon it, she'd finally caught sight of that single word, which now held the gravity of all her hopes inside each of its four letters... *"PASS!"*

At last, all the months of studying- had paid off! All that dedication, commitment, and hard work had led her to something of an achievement. Even amongst life's many changing distractions; even amongst all the confusing new redirections... she'd realised; it was all worth it, as she jumped for joy and whizzed around the living room; screaming triumphantly, at the top of her voice-

"I passed! I passed! I paaaaaaassed!" whilst swinging her mother around.

"Offo! Acha! Acha beta! *(Good! Good Daughter!)* Bus ker ub! Mai Girjowungi! *(That's enough now! I'll fall!)*." her mother cried out, filled with joy and slight terror.

With an instant urge to run straight to Inder's house and tell him; without even a second's thought; she was already running as fast as her feet could carry her and hurtling towards his house with her fist- as if on autopilot; already ready to knock loudly and persistently upon his front door! But then came that all too familiar- fall from grace! When a grim-faced Hema opened the door and instantly extinguished all her former exhilaration!

"I ummm... I ummm... He, Hema I umm... In, Inder, is he ho... home?" Sudesh stuttered, struggling to speak, with Hema knowingly glaring at her.

"No!" Hema retorted; before promptly slamming the front door shut in Sudesh's face.

Walking back to her house; feeling wholly deflated, foolish, and utterly embarrassed; her eyes were now firmly fixed on the grey pavement- she walked; as any remaining excitement melted away with the passing breeze. But, approaching her, she noticed a familiar pair of highly polished, brown leather shoes! *It was him!* She looked up, as warmth filled her insides and as she saw his face... *his beautiful face...* he was sunshine! He stood with his broad and knowing smile; he looked deep into her eyes. She desperately wanted to embrace him and scream joyfully and spin him around. But she knew she couldn't, and she knew she shouldn't! Nonetheless, the moment was caught inside a beautiful and undeniable serendipity; finally, they were face to face and sharing such an open and honest smile between them—no more games.

"Pass- Madam?" He asked, cocking his head to one side.

"Pass- Sir!" She replied, cocking her head back at him.

With their smiles lingering in the air, they crossed opposite paths, simultaneously walking back to their own homes and both turning back momentarily; to take in that one long last look at each other before entering their homes. Both were acutely aware it might be the last time they saw one another. At least, for some time to come and unsure; when, where, and how they'd ever meet again!

HIDING IN PLAIN SIGHT

"Better to live one year as a tiger, than a hundred as a sheep" Madonna

That weekend, to celebrate her exam result, the rest of The Seths gathered to enjoy some deep-fried spicy samosas and freshly churned milk lassis *(shakes)* while their father was out. Unbeknownst to Sudesh, Raj had also invited her *private tutor* to the shindig! Suddenly, seeing Inder walk into the living room; almost made her choke on her milk lassi! The first time he'd visited, since they'd become *more* than just friends, she felt elated and terrified seeing him and instantly on tenter-hooks. Trying her best to act as calmly as possible, even whilst her insides spasmed with dread and anxiety, she wondered *why he'd not declined the invitation- knowing it would be unbearable to manage!* But with the viable excuse of formally congratulating his clever little student, Inder had shown up like a brave, if not *stupid*, mouse entering a lion's den! Thoughtfully bringing with him; a large box of her favourite Indian sweets as if in compensation for his incorrigible audacity!

"Wow! Motichoor Ladoos! *(Sweet gram flour dessert balls!)* How did you know that these are Sudesh's- favourite?" Raj innocently enquired as he excitedly grabbed the extra-large box and started distributing almost the entire contents amongst Sudesh's greedy siblings; before she'd even got a look in!

"Oh… umm… just a wild guess!" Inder coyly replied, smirking at Sudesh; as he took his jacket off.

Though they tried their hardest to avoid inspiring suspicion and proceeded with caution by purposefully avoiding one another and dispersing whenever in close proximity, they'd inadvertently managed to achieve the opposite effect. Their concerted efforts; only made them appear unusually nervous, unnaturally awkward, and over-formal with one another. Instead, they looked more as if they'd had a falling out! And it wasn't long before someone noticed and questioned their strange behaviour!

"Sudesh? Uh... has Inder upset you over something?" Raj questioned a nervous-looking Sudesh.

"Huh? Oh... No! Why? Why do you ask?" She tried her darndest to appear calm, loudly gulping down the frog in her throat alongside the ice-cold lassi and giving herself an instant brain freeze!

"Oh, it's nothing, just you both seem a bit... strange," he responded, looking confused.

"Strange!? No!... us? No! Not at all!" She nervously replied before darting away from him.

Now feeling even more paranoid, she impulsively tried to over-compensate, strutting towards Inder and catching him off guard- mid-conversation with her brother- Billu. Suddenly, she burst out into laughter beside them; as they both stopped and looked at her. With growing confusion on their faces, they both wondered- what the sudden joke was. Feeling increasingly nervous, she tried desperately to explain; by blurting out the first thing that came into her head!

"Oh! ...umm... Inder... umm... I was laughing because... my Mumma was asking if... if... if you want more samosas! But I said No! Of course, he doesn't! He doesn't want to get fat!" she laughed nervously.

She spat out her nonsense; before realising- just how stupid it sounded- given that he still held a plate full of samosas in his hands! - she again started to laugh nervously before glaring dagger eyes at Inder! As if trying to prompt him into somehow *helping her!* Finally clocking on, he too began nervously laughing as a devastating awkwardness took hold and as everyone appeared to stop what they were doing; to look right at them! All sharing the same expression of confusion and as if all wondering the same thing- '... whether someone had secretly spiked their cold lassis, with bung! *(Cannabis!)*' With her head getting lighter and her cheeks; suddenly burning around the accumulated droplets of sweat; she quickly rushed off towards the kitchen; realising, in her efforts to act normal; she was, instead, acting like a complete and utter lunatic!

LIGHT BULB

After a few long and painful days apart, they became increasingly desperate to see one another again. Sat alone in his study- hours on end; he'd stare into space and reminisce upon their moments, the memories as if etched onto the bare walls surrounding him. She'd continually be drawn to her front door and windows, watching his house for any signs of him, and each time, she would catch a momentary glimpse of his face... *his beautiful face*; her heart would skip a beat, and she'd have to fight her deep desire to run straight to him and leave behind all her inhibitions and fears. Falling into his arms and staying there, carefree within his embrace, as the world melted away around them and until- forcibly pried apart. Imagining his arms around her again was such sweet bliss; it was worth any thrashing that might follow!

One morning, putting his washed and ironed clothes away into his cupboard, Inder spotted a little rip on the arm of one of his favourite shirts. With no sewing skills- himself and unkeen to ask his mother or sisters for help; he suddenly remembered- how good Sudesh was at *sewing*, and with that, a lightbulb went off in his head, together with an ingenious idea! Turning up at The Seth's house, wearing his ripped shirt, he pretended as if he'd popped by to visit Raj whilst his eagle eyes continually scanned; in search of his lover! And, when Sudesh walked into the living room, it was like time had stood still. Both, instantly fighting that magnetised pull towards one another, and that desperate desire to hold an extended gaze. Almost having gasped aloud upon seeing Inder sat in her living room- as if butter wouldn't melt in his mouth; Sudesh tried again to hide her terror and excitement from showing on her face! She'd always envied Inder's ability to look calm and in control in situations like this! Especially when being around him made every fibre of her being; scream aloud on high alert, and even the most straightforward task of breathing- so challenging! After the quickest of 'hellos' under her breath, she excused herself back into the kitchen to continue helping her mother prepare tea. With her heartbeat racing, alongside the million thoughts running through her head, she wondered- *what Inder was doing there? Why had he suddenly turned up, unannounced and uninvited like this?* With her nerves in tatters, she struggled to focus on anything she was doing, and even keeping a grip on the bowl of her mother's freshly fried onion bhajis was impossible as she clumsily dropped a whole load onto the dusty floor.

"Oh, Shit!" She exclaimed, quickly bending down and trying to retrieve them; right before her mother came and slapped them straight back out of her hands again!

"Offo! Dhyaan se! *(Carefully!)* Leave them! Kharaab ho gae! *(They are bad!)* Ja, jaldee se baakee ke le ja *(Go, quickly take the rest!)*." Her mother impatiently instructed as she collected the onion bhajis from the floor to throw out.

"It's ripped, Yaar! *(Mate!)*" Sudesh heard Raj say to Inder as she entered the living room again and started clumsily serving the tea, as her racing pulse throbbed in her flushed face.

"Huh?" Inder asked, acting oblivious- "What is ripped?"

"Your shirt! It's ripped. Look. Your sleeve, see?" Raj pointed at the tear on Inder's shirt sleeve.

"Oh...Yes... yes, of course it is! Look at that!" Inder innocently exclaimed.

"Eh!... give it to Sudesh? She will sew it up. She's very good at sewing!" Raj casually suggested on Sudesh's behalf just as she looked at Inder and caught his strange smirk.

"Oh no, no its ok... I wouldn't want to trouble her," he benevolently replied.

"It's cool, Yaar! *(Mate!)* Give it. She'll do a quick fix. She loves to sew! As much as you love bhajis!" Raj teasingly insisted, nudging Inder playfully, as Inder stuffed his mouth with a hot bhaji, and Raj left to wash his hands.

Sudesh looked at Inder with dagger eyes as he suddenly stood up, a glint of victory in his eyes, and casually started to take his shirt off! "What! What the hell? What are you doing? What game are you playing?" she whispered loudly in a panic.

"Game? No game, sweetheart... just taking my shirt off... for yooooou!" he sang his words teasingly at her, childishly chuckling away.

"What? Oh my God! Why are you here? Stop! Stop taking your shirt off!" she tried stopping him, to no avail! "Look! We've already made everyone suspicious- last time you came with your bloody *Ladoo's!*" she continued with urgency, trying her best to ignore how handsome he looked- standing there, with nothing on his chest beside his white vest!

"Oh... but I thought mothichoor ladoos, was your favourite...?" he teased as she smacked his arm. "Great! So, you are not even happy to see me?" he teased her childishly.

"Hey, Bhagavaan! *(Oh God!)* Shush! Shuuuuush pleeeeease!" she insisted, stepping away from him; just before catching the sound of Raj's, returning footsteps!

"It's ok! ... trust me! I have a plan! Wait and watch how awesomely my mind works, meri jaan! *(My love!)*" He quickly whispered before Raj walked back in.

Handing her his shirt and secretly winking as she shuddered with dread and snatched it from him, Inder returned to his seat. Panic building inside her; like a fizzy bottle about to pop, she rushed away to fetch her sewing kit as her mother walked in with a large colander full of vegetables.

"Oh, Namaste *(Hello)* Inder beta! *(Son!)*" her mother greeted Inder cheerfully before sighing and sitting down to cut her vegetables.

"Namaste *(Hello)* Aunti ji... Namaste! *(Hello!)*" Inder responded confidently before loudly slurping his tea and watching Sudesh return holding her sewing kit.

"You know what...?" Inder suddenly said, as Sudesh's heart almost stopped.

Oh my God! What will he say next? she desperately wondered!

"I was just thinking... now that Sudesh has passed..." he spoke so calmly as her insides exploded, oppositely, from him merely mentioning her name!

Nervously sat down on the floor with her legs crossed; she started to sew his shirt, desperately afraid of what he might say next. Keeping one eye on her sewing and the other firmly on him, she waited with bated breath!

"Maybe, she could go on to college now? I heard there is an excellent Stitching diploma at the local college..." Inder continued, intermittently slurping his tea and unashamedly helping himself to fresh hot onion bhajis, one after the next.

"Really?" Raj's interest was piqued; as he bit into his bhaji and blew the steam out of his mouth.

"I think- it's always good- especially for a *girl*... you know... to learn such skills- to a high standard," Inder shrugged, biting into another hot bhaji, and navigating the steam, from its hot batter.

Getting more and more irritated; not least by his sexist comments and the fact that she'd imagined achieving a tad more in life- than simply *good sewing skills*; she listened on intently; hanging off his every word, and so distracted that she accidentally pricked the sewing needle, into her index finger!

"Ouch!" She squirmed, looking at the pin drop of blood on her fingertip.

"You- ok?" Inder asked with sudden concern before checking himself and returning calmly to his bhaji.

"Offo! Bhagavaan jaane is ladakee ka damaag kahaan hai! *(Oh my! God knows where this girl's brain is!)*." her mother retorted, with little sympathy and growing annoyance, at Sudesh's lack of concentration.

On this bloody idiot!... Who else? Sudesh felt like shouting aloud as she sucked the tiny spec of blood on her fingertip and eyeballed Inder again.

"Some even say... it can help a girl get better matches... for *marriage*, I mean!" He candidly added as he secretly smirked at Sudesh, who was now fuming beneath her embarrassed smile!

Loudly clearing her throat, Sudesh warned Inder off, wishing she could walk straight up to him and slap him across his smug face! Instead, she just breathed deeply and prayed- *Please, God! Please let there be a sensible point- to the rubbish coming out of this man's mouth!*

"Maybe, it might also help her get a well-paid- *lady's type* job!" He slyly added, before shrugging his shoulders, as if to demonstrate it was merely a passing thought.

But Sudesh knew that nothing with Inder was ever inconsequential! He was far too clever for that. He always had a hidden agenda and said what needed to be said, nothing more! Even his sly little throwaway comments were always tinged with a hidden meaning or a certain point. And although she couldn't help but feel annoyed by his rather sexist and old-fashioned attitude and comments, and as much as she felt like- wringing his neck, she knew there must be more to it. After another moment's reflection, she then had her own epiphany and little lightbulb moment, suddenly realising; just what he was up to!

"Oh, yes! Good idea, Yaar! *(Mate!)* Dekho na mumma, *(Look mum)* how clever my friend's brain works!" Raj proudly declared, oblivious to the invisible knife; his friend held at his back.

Undoubtedly impressed by Inder's courage and calculated foresight, she quickly caught on to the fact that Inder was scheming to get her- out of the house! It was merely a means to an end! Once she'd finished the last stitch on his shirt, she walked up to him and handed it back.

"Here you go! It is done!" she snapped.

"Yes. It is done!" He knowingly responded. "Wow! you do certainly have... *skillful* hands!" He smirked as he picked another onion bhaji and ate it. "Mumm! Mmm! Mmm! Vah! Vah! Vah! *(Wow! Wow! Wow!)* Aunty ji- kya svaad svaad pakode banae hain! *(What delicious onion bhajis these are!)* I have eaten too many! Definitely, I would be fat if I lived here!" he chuckled.

Although Sudesh had no idea; how the logistics of Inder's plan would work, she was quietly confident- that Inder, being Inder, would undoubtedly have it all in hand! Besides, she was fully aware of her family's vested interest in preparing the females for the best marriage offers and getting well-paid *lady-type* jobs! Inder sure was a master manipulator, and had she not loved him; she'd have hated him for it instead!

HOOK, LINE AND SINKER!

Days on, hearing all her family discussing the sewing course at length and complimenting Inder for his '...kind and helpful nature' certainly made her feel proud and slightly guilty! Even her father had fallen for Inder's clever charm offensive. He, too, was none the wiser to his ulterior motives, which, far from being altruistic, duped everyone into a false sense of security. But even though they knew all this and what a considerable risk they were taking, neither could deny the forbidden fruit's *sweet* taste. Quenching their immediate thirst and desires, it helped obscure reality and blurred any visions and worries of the future. Right now, all that mattered was being together. The pain of being apart; was too hard to bear, and their magnets' pull was almost crippling. Deciding to live in the moment, they thanked their lucky stars that for now, at least, everyone had fallen for Inder's bate- hook, line, and sinker!

FIVE-POINT PLAN

1. The inconspicuous couple would meet both before and after sewing classes.
2. She would relay extended start and finish times- for her course; to facilitate meetings.
3. He would pick and drop her from around the corner of their houses- before and after his work shifts.
4. They would navigate Inder's work shifts and her college days, break times, and days off- to meet as much as possible.
5. They'd frequent restaurants, parks, cinemas, shops, and tea houses; out of their local area and, when necessary, use Santosh as a trusted alibi! And on the surface, at least, it was the most perfect plan!

SABOTAGE

Things took a turn for the worse; when suddenly, Sudesh's arched rival sister Indu, also decided she wanted in! '...why should I miss out? I want better marriage offers- too!' She brazenly and persuasively argued! Forever in competition with her sisters and encouraged by the rest of her family, it was suddenly decided that both sisters would now enrol at the college for the sewing course! And with that, the star-crossed lovers found themselves in yet another conundrum! A week later, as the two sisters, arrived at the local college, Sudesh was baffled on how to proceed; knowing her and Inder's- previously well-laid plans; were being sabotaged right under their nose, and there was little they could do to stop it!

"Eh! What is wrong with you today?" Indu had naively enquired, after noticing her sister's foul mood.

She wished dearly; she could confide and reason with her sister. But she knew Indu, could not be trusted. Especially not with the weight of such a huge secret, like that of a *forbidden* love affair!

"You- on your period, or something!" Indu impatiently probed, as Sudesh huffed and puffed hastily in front of her, rushing towards the college.

"Yes! ...Yes, I am!" Sudesh snapped, aptly using the little lie to cover her strange mood.

"Oi! What's the hurry? Slow down Nareeee!" Indu shouted, fighting to keep up and knowing full well- calling her that; was her achilleas heal!

"Don't call me that- stupid! I hate that! Keep up, or go home, I don't care what you do!" Sudesh growled, like a petulant child.

LUCKY SPOT

Fate finally started to conspire on the couple's behalf-when the sewing diploma course turned out; more popular than anticipated. With a room full of would-be female candidates equally eager to sign up and similarly intent on increasing their chances for good marriage proposals, the competition suddenly revved up a notch!

However, it soon became apparent- that those girls, from seemingly more affluent families, were leaving with application forms- one after another, and yet, girls from seemingly poorer ones; were leaving empty-handed! Needless to say- Indu, who was dressed modestly in her shabby old Indian suit, was informed that- the course was full. Yet somewhat surprisingly, when Sudesh; who'd also not made any concerted efforts with her appearance- asked for a form; she was instantly handed it, alongside having her name ticked off upon the course's provisional list. But little did either one of them realise; that Inder had, yet again, worked his midas touch alongside a bit of nepotism and called in favour with a friend- a friend- who just happened to be on the admissions board! So, as soon as Sudesh gave her full name, a place suddenly became available, especially for her, and as if by magic!

"I just don't understand!" a perplexed Indu protested, racking her brain and trying to make sense of it "...it does not make sense! How come they said *yes* to you but *no*- to me? And you went in after me!"

"Maybe I got lucky!" Sudesh slyly replied, as her mind started to join the dots... "but at least one of us got in!" she smugly continued, trying her hardest to appear sympathetic under her faintly forming grin!

"Huh! That's easy for you to say, Nareeee!" Indu snapped before storming off back toward home.

13

FORBIDDEN FRUIT

"Forbidden fruit is the sweetest"

They met regularly. On occasion, Inder would take a day off work, and Sudesh would bravely forge her mother's signature- to provide sick notes for her teacher. Life was filled with abundant joy, excitement, and intoxicatingly carefree bliss. It surrounded them like a warm blanket and kept them snugly inside this nomad's land, where they were both cocooned from the outside world. Both the happiest and the riskiest days, they were swept up on the wings of their desires, sucking on their slushed iced Gola's whilst walking the edges of lakes and cuddling beneath the shade of the neem trees. Having naively assumed if they could only keep their gaze upon one another and turn away from the outside world, it would be enough to deny and block it out completely.

In the blink of an eye, a whole year flew past, enveloped in the cascades of this blossoming romance and living every moment apart in bated anticipation of seeing one another again. Nothing else and no one else mattered anymore. However, as the year-long course neared its end, Time- the fickle mistress; was quickly running out on them, and somehow, unbeknownst to them; their luck had run out on them, too! Soon, far too soon, they'd be harshly reawakened from that sweet lover's dream!

NEWSFLASH!

'Inder and Sudesh have been secretly meeting! They are more than just friends!'

The tongues came wagging, sparking a wildfire and igniting a firestorm! On one tumultuous evening, they were each confronted and verbally and physically attacked by their infuriated families. Far from denying things; both were too tired to protest the allegations; instead, they unashamedly admitted their undying love for one another; sparking even more anger and fury! But both families; remained adamant- '...this relationship would never be accepted! And was not permitted to continue even a second longer!' And with that, the couple had been *forbidden* from ever speaking and meeting again! This mutual decision proved to be the only thing the two sides would ever agree on!

CUT TIES

Though they lived opposite and passed by frequently, the two sides completely refrained from speaking to each other. Raj and Indu's friendships with Inder and Hema also faced a bitter end. Overnight, the couple had gone from their lover's dream into the worst-imaginable- living nightmare! That previously soft and warm cocoon of love had quickly been replaced by cold, suffocating brick walls! With zero contact, they'd been cut off, not just from one another, but also from the outside world. Bar Inder- going to his job and returning home; they remained grounded within their respective houses and even stopped speaking with any of their friends over the phone, many of whom had been suspected of aiding this secret love affair behind the elder's backs!

SOLITUDE

"The past is never dead. It's not even past" William Faulkner

She woke every morning with the same deep drowning feeling of dread in the pit of her stomach, alongside that same hollow and stagnant void gripping the insides of her chest. She'd stopped looking at her clock or calendar and bar the que from sunrise and sunset; from the light and darkness formed around the window and doors; it felt like an eternal night was now within. In any case, it was of little significance- when one had nowhere to go and nothing to do besides chores! Which had now been increased in volume to occupy any idle time. Her days folded into one another, inside a perpetually endless prism of time- which felt ceaseless, unremitting, and continued, even whilst all else had seemingly stopped.

Her butterflies and their invisible flutters were now just a distant echo, like a dream from the past. Her longing, so desperate for so long, was replaced by impassive apathy and complete withdrawal from life itself. Now, she existed in a disconnected and unplugged state, as an absolute nothingness took over. Even her butterflies had surrendered; quietly shrivelled and shrunken, they lay dormant inside a comatose state as if they resided in time's decay. Her relentless tears, which had tirelessly and pointlessly poured out of her vacant eyes like dripping taps, were now all but dried up, leaving behind taught remnants of salted lines in the painful deep scores across her face. Everything detritus, just a composite of remnants and debris of her past, left amongst the residual reminders of once having felt wanted, once having been loved and cherished, and once having felt fully alive.

She'd not looked in a mirror for so long and could barely remember the last time she'd bothered to wash. Like a snake's peel ready to shed, her skin somehow hung on stubbornly to her bones, and her tangled, matted locks were like rotten leaves mushed together and stuck to her oily scalp. Everything, everywhere, was now a reflection of her innate defeat. She had to force herself to eat and drink and, sometimes, even force herself to breathe.

Hours spent; lying and staring at the familiar decaying paint upon the same old drabby ceilings and walls, hovering around her with impending doom. She'd learnt all their shapes, the contoured light and shaded parts, every little crack, crevice, and bulge, studying them obsessively and recalling every tiny detail; before entering the closed tunnels of her eyes each night, hoping to escape another day somehow. Desperately trying to think of anything but him! Anything but his touch and his face... his beautiful, beautiful face... His tormenting memory, now like a slow poison inside her veins, brought her ever closer to the edge of life and the doorways of death! The stone surrounding her; was like a suffocating bouldered coffin, and the limiting space, as if turning inwards and wilting in like a dying flower. She was now just an empty vessel; floating like a ghostly shadow upon a pier; hovering above the jagged rocks, shrouded in dismay; just waiting for the waves to come crashing in and carry her deep into its eternal dark shores.

LIGHT

"When the world pushes you to your knees, you're in the perfect position to pray" Rumi

The last voice she'd expected to hear on the other side of her bedroom door was that of a friend! For a moment, she'd assumed it was simply a figment of her imagination and yet another voice; trapped inside her head, amongst all the clustered images, which tricked her grasp upon reality and sent her hazy head ever closer towards the beckoning descent of insanity.

"Sudeeeeeeesh!" came the hushed voice again.

Then, as the dawn of day shone through the edges of her closed bedroom door, she suddenly realised; this voice was real!

"Sudesh! Can you hear me? Sudessssh?"

Forcing her eyes open, she lifted her heavy, led-like being from the moulded outline on her mattress. It seemed that after a month of pleading- Santosh had finally convinced Sudesh's mother to allow her to visit. Even if only for a few minutes and courtesy of her clever excuse of- needing to collect study books-she'd previously lent Sudesh. Luckily, it worked, and she was permitted access past the heavily guarded checkpoints of The Seth's house!

"Santosh!?" Sudesh called out, "Is that you? Is it really you?"

"Yes! Yes, it is me! But I do not have long!" Santosh hollered back, "I have a message!" she continued before suddenly lowering her voice into a loud whisper "...from In... Inder!" she added; while fumbling with her bag and taking out her own books- to look like they'd been collected from Sudesh!

And all she had heard was that single word, that name- which effectively pulled her out of her former descent, capturing her fullest attention... *Inder!* Suddenly, it was as if a power supply of electricity had plugged her back to life again as she jumped out of her jaded slumber and ran her horribly stiff legs towards her bedroom door. Before, it was flung open, and they both looked upon one another, stunned! Sudesh fell into Santosh's arms, forcing her to drop all the books again. Santosh hugged Sudesh's skeletal frame, almost afraid she might break her friend; should she apply too much pressure- given how much weight she'd lost!

"Oh my God- Sudesh! What have you done to yourself? Oh, Maaa! *(Oh, mother!)* You have lost too much weight! You must eat!" Santosh cried out in alarm.

"Oh, Santosh! Oh, Santosh!" Sudesh sobbed on her friend's shoulder.

After hearing oncoming footsteps, Santosh suddenly hunched over onto the floor to retrieve her books. Although she wanted to hug and console her friend longer, she knew there was no time to waste, and she must get right to the point; before someone showed up!

"I'm so sorry, Sudesh. I do not have long! I must tell you his message... before someone comes! Your mother only allowed me in for one minute! To collect my books back! Well, at least, pretend to!" She scoffed.

"Yes, ok... What? What did he say? It's over, isn't it?" Sudesh whispered with growing panic as more tears ran down her tightly sore cheeks and stung her raw red skin.

"No! No, of course not! He still loves you! He said to tell you- he misses you greatly! He cannot live without you! And he will never give up! And- you, too- must not give up! Ok? I can't stay! Can you believe- I now have to take my books back! Offo! The things I do... for you both! Thoba! Thoba! *(Goodness! Goodness!)*" Santosh laughed nervously as she rolled her eyes and shook her head in dismay.

"But... but..." Sudesh interrupted. She wanted more!

"Shush!" Santosh suddenly stopped her, "I think... I can hear someone coming! Ok, I must go! I'll try to come back again soon! Promise! Promise me; you will Eat!? You must eat! Hey Ram! *(God- help!)*"

14

PHOENIX

"Love is not love which alters it when alteration finds, or bends with the remover to remove O no!... love alters not with his brief hours and weeks, but bears it out, even to the edge of doom" (Sonnet 116) William Shakespeare

FIGHT

Knowing Inder's affections hadn't been tarnished by his family's disapproval and rejection and that he'd not caved in under pressure and expectations; bought her renewed hope. When she hadn't heard from him, she'd started to doubt him, his love, and his intentions. But now her faith was restored at the pivotal juncture when her abandoning existence had almost drifted too far away from home and from him. Previously, it had always been Inder who was the brave, courageous one who saw beyond limitations and obstacles and always sought a way. But now she, too, was finding courage, within his courage; strength within his strength, and she realised their love was worth fighting for. Her first fight was with herself and her desire to throw caution to the wind and slam her adrenaline-filled body straight through her bedroom door and bulldozer her way into Inder's arms. But with her newfound courage also came some wisdom, which cautioned her not to do anything rash and to play instead- the long game. So instead of rushing to escape from her cage, she decided to sit and wait for the calm and to hold fast to her faith in him and his love. Then, as she calmed, she listened to that inner guiding voice, reassuring her that... *all would be ok. All would somehow work out in the end, especially now that she knew; he was waiting!* A tiny flickering light appeared at the end of that very dark tunnel. Absorbing focus into her wait, she would stay put until a true sign came and until she could see a complete path, clearing. At which point, she would charge ahead in blind courage. She would run down that path as if running for dear life, like the mightiest gust of wind. Feeling both a sense of relief and torment, she cried. She cried and cried until her tears ran out and then decided... *she would not cry anymore!* And just like that, just like any great love story, something more powerful had now taken over. Something, which felt almost out of her control now, stirred up inside her like a building storm. Little embers sparked up and ignited themselves; as if to born- a new wildfire, which could burn anything in its path. Like a phoenix rising from the ashes, it readied her for an almighty fight alongside a most venturesome flight!

UPRISING

With the coming of a new season; also came a brand-new dawn filled with sweet hope. Simmering inside each of their marooned hearts- from right across the street, it burned brighter and brighter each day. Each night, their tortured souls yearned for one another; while staring at the same stars, burning inside the same black skies and each mourning, they grew bolder and bolder; within the blistering sunrise. With each passing day, it felt like the universe itself; was beginning to resonate inside their breaths. Like the universe was somehow responding to their new-found frequencies; in the wake of their inescapable wills. Finally, she was permitted to return to college and leave her former cage. Yet, an uprising surged from within, even within the strictest times and under the many watchful eyes escorting her guarded chastity around the realms. Simply stepping beyond her bricked-up threshold made her toes tingle in excitement and made her feet want to tap dance; upon promised pastures anew. She realised that the more her feet were held back and bound, the more they ached to step up, step on and step away. The more she was withheld, the more she wanted to break free. The more barriers and obstacles put in her path, the more compelling it felt for her to jump, gallop, and absconder far beyond her restricted boundary.

WARRIORS

"Of all the roads she traveled, the journey back to herself was the most magnificent" Ledo Grand

And across the street, he, too, was riling inside his ignited uprising. He, too, realised that; the more their love was forsaken, sacrificed, and denied, the more it deepened the possession of their hearts, minds, and wills. The more they were expected to quietly and obediently abandon and relinquish their desires, the more incandescent they became to do the very opposite! Each had decided in themselves that if needed, they'd shout and scream from the very rooftops of their youth and demand their love's vindication. They'd renounce their former victimhood and challenge any fate, striving for greater justice. They'd decided to live even harder, love even deeper, burn even brighter, and aerate their love with even more oxygen than before with each remaining breath. This forbidden fruit they'd so perilously craved for so long would now be devoured at any cost! Each day passing inside bated enslavement; would only help to tighten their bond and bind their unification inside an even more formidable conviction- *that somehow, someday, and in some way, they would justify their love. Their love was not weak and defenceless, and they were no longer simply victims of their fate... instead, their love was limitless and boundless, and they were Fucking Warriors!*

SECRET CODE

In the days and weeks that followed, a few messages were passed between them via trusted friends like Santosh or a rather ingenious secret coded sign language system they'd developed over time. Whenever they'd spot one another on their adjacent balconies, they'd scratch various body parts to communicate simple messages. Although most often, Inder was the only one who dared communicate like this, even while in close proximity to his siblings and parents!

A scratch on the forehead- 'Hello!' A scratch on the cheek- 'I miss you!' And a scratch on the chest- 'I love you!' It's a wonder; no one ever caught on, or at least became concerned with their sudden strange skin afflictions, given all the relentless scratching! Occasionally, Inder would tie up a little love note around a small pebble or stone and throw it onto Sudesh's balcony. Fortunately, being an accomplished bowler meant that he had naturally good aim! Each time, he'd prewarn her by scratching the top of his head; sending her into an instant panic-filled excitement; as she'd suddenly start rushing around; trying to grab hold of it before someone noticed or got to it first! Nonetheless, these thoughtful little love notes often proved the highlight of her tedious days and reassured her- that he'd not forgotten or forsaken her. With only a small space upon which to write, he'd often resort to sweet little abbreviated words like- 'U r mine, Love u, Meri Jaan, Miss u, Hugs, kisses, always us and, only u' And on those days when Sudesh appeared, particularly down, he'd send notes saying- 'Soon! Be happy!', or simply- 'Smile!' and each note, always finished with his signature- 'X,' signifying his loving kiss.

CHANCED SIGHTINGS

With the final semester of her sewing course nearing its end, the couple had barely seen each other for weeks. After the big storm- created from their ousting, all that remained were chanced sightings, either whilst out shopping or across their respective windows, doors, and balconies. On the rare occasion when they'd stumble across one another alone, they'd keep their exchanges brief, consumed with the fear of prying eyes- reporting back to their families and starting another storm of arguments. They'd come to realise that amongst all the seemingly friendly faces and confidantes, there were some hidden enemies of their love too! Not least, envious adversaries with insatiable appetites for gossip and a tendency for stirring pots, which served up deadly stews!

MILK MAID

Once her course had ended, Sudesh swiftly acquired a part-time position as a maid at the local milk depot. Her four-hour shifts, split into two hours every morning and two hours every afternoon, provided a small window of opportunity within which the couple tried to see one another. Although most of the time, they'd barely catch a quick glimpse of one another's faces- from a far and safe distance; on the rarest occasions, they'd manage an actual chat before abruptly parting ways again; after having spotted a suspicious onlooker. Conducting; themselves with great caution and as if part of a secret service covert operation, every sighting, every conversation, and every interaction; always needed to be as discreet and brief as possible; to avoid attracting unnecessary attention. However, even against all these efforts to remain inconspicuous, it wasn't long before a nosey neighbour; inevitably spotted them and ousted them yet again! Yet again, igniting an uproar of arguments, threats, and sanctions upon them. Now, with every little move and interaction being scrutinised even more, the many eyes of the many hawks endlessly followed and monitored them, and even that little interaction they'd previously had, was now stifled.

ESCORTS

Forbidden from going out anywhere unsupervised, Sudesh was again kept under lock and key by her family. Assigned with endless escorts everywhere she went, she was now only ever permitted to leave home for work. As time went on, feeling more and more frustrated and suffocated, her incendiary mood lent to frequent angry outbursts, often followed by regular thrashings- '...Helloooow? Doesn't anyone want to escort me to the shower? Don't you want to join me- in the toilet? Look, I'm going aaaaall by myself! Aaaaall alone! God knows what might happen! Where I might suddenly vanish too! Come? You have to check! Make sure I don't disappear!' She'd sarcastically taunt them. With her patience running thinner, weeks passed by without so much as setting eyes upon Inder, even from afar. And as the colder weather settled in, even his little love notes on her balcony had stopped. Now, all she could do was sit on the other side of her locked windows and doors and pray for a single little glimpse of him just to know that he was ok. Just to know- he was still *alive!* Soon, she even struggled to conjure his face inside her mind's eye, at least not as vividly as she once could. Noticing the decline in her mental state and low moods, some of her family tried to cheer her up by diverting her attention away from Inder and her past. However futile it seemed, they wanted to inspire her to focus on her future without him. But without him, she couldn't see anything but darkness. Their ignorant remarks; only served to frustrate and annoy her even further and push her away from them even more. With her heart utterly broken and her wings fully clipped, she wondered how anyone could ever expect her to live and love again, let alone fulfill her dreams of one day flying free.

MESSENGER PIGEONS

He, however, remained undeterred. Forever the optimist, he could never easily accept defeat and give up. Instead, he used his spare time to plan and plot even more, navigating ingenious ways to communicate with her, if not simply keep a check on her. Via his far-reaching social circle of friends- who'd happily come to his aid as willing secret messenger pigeons; he sent random people to her; to deliver secret messages on his behalf.

Often turning up at her workplace; the messengers came in many shapes and sizes and from all walks of life; pretending to be her family friends, if not simply new customers; seeking fresh pails of milk! Sometimes, she'd even mistake a regular customer- for a secret messenger and end up making silly fow-pars, confusing them with her strange conversations, if not accidentally handing them secret love notes! But eventually, Inder found a solution for this problem, too; when he instructed all his messengers- to use designated code words like- 'Lemonade!' and 'Biscuit!' to help identify themselves; before going on to relay any messages. With Inder's sweet promises held tightly at her breast, she spent all her time consumed in anticipation of his wonderful messenger pigeons and the pieces of paper they bought, filled with inks of hope.

FACES IN THE CROWD

Out with her family members, running errands, she'd occasionally spot Inder in the far-off distance or amongst crowds of strangers. His face; always appeared like an apparition and instantly made her heart race. Held hostage inside her desperate desire; to run straight to him; each time, she'd have to physically stop herself and fight off every cell in her body; which ached and pulled towards him. She'd often had to bury her feelings and ignore him, acting like he was a stranger and as if they were merely passing ships at sea. Within seconds, it would seem as if he was right there before her and then suddenly vanished and gone! Sometimes, she'd wonder whether; *she'd imagined him being there. Or if her desperate mind; was playing tricks on her?* Other times, even when she couldn't see him physically before her, she'd get such a strong sense of him and his presence; that it would feel as if he was secretly watching over her, like her very own guardian angel.

WAVES

In the coming months, suspicions would rise and falter like waves about whether Sudesh and Inder were still in contact. Whenever the waves of suspicion would rise- the families would all tighten their reins around the couple and start to monitor their every little move carefully. However, whenever the waves of suspicion would instead falter, the couple would be ready, like perfidious opportunists, pushing back on their boundaries and exploiting any little window of opportunity. Besides, the mass coordination of surveillance, befallen upon their adversaries, was proving quite exhausting and frustrating- for all concerned. Moreover, the concerted effort to keep tabs on the couple's every movement gradually grated on Sudesh's siblings, most of all! They'd started to resent not only the added responsibility and inconvenience of babysitting her but also the apparent invasion of their privacy and their schedules, and therein... would lay the couple's *Golden Opportunity!*

HEMA WEDS

A few weeks later, Hema was married! Sudesh and her family intermittently observed the week-long fanfare from the safe distance of their living room windows. Each one- trying to watch the festivities and events as discreetly as possible and each; dispersing and acting uninterested; whenever someone else entered the living room. None more so than Sudesh, who couldn't wait to see the back of Hema's sour face! Watching gleefully as Hema was being prepared for her final leave; she sat like a Christmas tree inside her traditional Doli cart; covered in sparkly tinsels and colourful flowers, with a gregarious percussion band; jauntily following behind and leading her away. The synchronized joy and relief; evident on many faces, especially Inder's! It was a spectacle to behold; both exhilaratingly loud and strangely emotional and something she'd imagined for herself; when she'd be sat inside her own beautifully decorated bridal Doli cart and escorted with triumphant fanfare, even if simply across the other side of the street! Now, all those previously intoxicating dreams; she'd once imagined; would remain just dreams! Simply imaginings of a young, naive, and innocent girl; who'd lost her grip on reality and been stupid enough to believe; her dreams were hers to claim and her destiny, hers to behold!

HIS FACE...

Finally, she saw his face... *his beautiful face...!* Also, seeming to be positively delighted about Hema's departure! (If his gleaming smile was anything to go by!) It indeed filled her heart, seeing him so happy and smiling, and yet, there was also a tiny part of her that resented seeing him so happy... so happy, without her! *How could he be laughing- so very joyfully and behave so playfully- without me?* She couldn't remember the last time she'd laughed and smiled so happily- without him! Now, seeing him rejoicing with his friends and relatives; seeing him dressed up handsome like a prospective groom; seeing those beautiful, embellished, and available girls- all dolled up like peacocks, swooning around him- as if ready to mate and ready to catch themselves a husband! - certainly made her feel pernicious, as well as slightly betrayed. With her butterflies fluttering in new anguish and her eyes burning in new envy, which she'd never experienced before- simply observing him like that... like that, without her; bought on a whole host of new emotions, not least, the ugly green eye of jealousy!

15

RUNAWAY

"You can only run away from a house. Home is something you run toward"

EXTRA *SPECIAL* MILK!

It was a swelteringly hot Thursday morning. As expected, she'd arrived at the milk depot promptly at 6 am. Whilst most others were still fast asleep, a choice few eager punters had already gathered, queuing since 5.30 am to collect their early morning rations of fresh milk. As she gradually made her way down the long line of people- pouring out liter-filled-ladle, after litre-filled-ladle, from her large churn into the seemingly endlessly appearing empty containers; she could feel herself falling into an almost rhythmically timed trance.

Just then, she caught sight of a strange old man, unusually shrouded for such a hot summer's day and trudging his frail body towards her as if being dragged through quicksand. More importantly, instead of joining the end of the queue, he headed straight for her, right to the front of the line, as if oblivious to the other people- already waiting! With his head staunchly bowed beneath his large black shawl, he'd instantly caused a stir with the other customers, who immediately started sighing and tutting at him. Before a few started calling out to him- trying to get his attention-

"Oh, ho!... Bapuji! *(Old man!)* Eh! Oi! Line lughi hai! Dekha nahin? *(There's a line here! Didn't you see?)* Hey! Oi! Hey?" they called out one after another. Their shared impatience quickly stamped out any former respect for his mature age!

However, instantly feeling sorry for him and having assumed that he must be hard of hearing, or else have dementia, if not-hiding an unfortunate deformity under his shroud, she instead ignored all the protests and decided to calmly serve him. Pouring out an extra generous ladle of milk, into his empty bucket; she was further surprised when even after his bucket was full and practically over spilling; he'd still not moved away! Instead, he stood there stubbornly, still holding his bucket towards her as if waiting for something else. Bewildered by this, she leaned in closer-

"Babaji... hello? Babaji? Dekho, mainne paadiya na, upke liye doodth- Dekho? *(Old man... hello? Old man? Look, I've put the milk for you- look?).*" she loudly, yet politely said to him.

"Lemonade!... Biscuit!" He suddenly whispered back at her in a strangely familiar voice!

It had been many weeks since she'd heard those code words or met with any secret messengers. And this one, in particular, seemed too old and frail; to be caught in such a task for Inder! With bated breath, she waited for a secret note to appear from under the old man's shroud. But instead, he suddenly startled her when he looked up at her from beneath his shawl and made her gasp aloud! Now, having spilled most of her next ladle of milk onto the floor, she had to do a double take- to ensure she wasn't seeing things! Unable to believe her own eyes, she'd almost fallen back when she saw the very last face, she'd expected to see on an otherwise regular Thursday morning at work!

It was him!... It was Inder!

"It's me!" he loudly whispered. "You silly idiot! Me! See!" He mockingly laughed, still half covered up, from the continually tutting crowd.

Taken aback, she stood there frozen momentarily, with her mouth wide open, looking at him! He smirked back at her with his familiar grin and teased her even further; by pulling a silly face at her! Then, relishing in the fact that he'd fooled her and suddenly feeling parched, he grabbed the ladle of milk off her and tried gulping down the contents- before she managed to yank it back, spilling the remainder of milk- which hadn't already reached his dribbling lips!

"W... what!... what are you doing? Why are you here?" She asked in a whispered panic, clocking all the prying eyes and ears, "...why are you dressed like an old man?" she asked, confused!

"Don't worry! Just listen carefully to me!" he whispered assertively, "It has all been arranged!"

"What has?" She asked.

"Our Wedding!" He grinned- ear to ear.

"Our what!?" She could barely believe her ears!

"We are getting married tomorrow!" He replied smugly, with excitement- beaming in his eyes.

She looked at him in shock and growing confusion, and before she could ask him anything else, he grabbed hold of her closer and spoke with immediate urgency.

"Just listen! However, you can do it- you must meet me tomorrow at 2 pm at the airfield! Please, Jaan! *(Love!)* I don't know what will happen- if my parents grab hold of my feet and beg me to marry somebody else... I might not be able to refuse them much longer! This is our only chance! 2 pm! Tomorrow! airfield!" He was almost ecstatic; as he quickly covered himself back up again and, without another word, suddenly darted off!

Running away with the unexpected sprint of an athlete, he left Sudesh utterly gobsmacked and the many confused onlookers, all wondering the very same thing... "How did that previously frail old man; suddenly become so very agile?... Maybe, there is something *extra* special... in this milkmaid's milk!"

RUNAWAY BRIDE!

The waves had faltered. Sudesh had been granted a couple of hours respite and permitted to visit with her friend Sarita straight after her morning shift. Raj planned to pick up Sudesh at 1 pm from work and drop her at Sarita's house. Before collecting her back at 3 pm, and bring her straight back home. *Her golden opportunity-* was to leave Sarita's house at 1.30 pm and pretend she would visit another friend- Radha (for whom nobody had a forwarding address or contact number!) Instead, she would go to the airfield and meet Inder by 2pm and then... run away to get married!

NOW- OR NEVER!

"Feet, what do I need you for when I have wings to fly?" Frida Kahlo

She took her time tucking in all her suit's edges, as discretely as possible, beneath her work suit. She held the most petite handbag, containing just a handful of money, her favourite pink lipstick, some tissues, and the magic keyring- Inder had gifted her. Her butterflies- fluttered in chaos as she checked the long mirror to ensure that her clothing didn't look too suspiciously bulky. Luckily, the thin fabrics lay nicely on her petite frame and were almost invisible even though they left her sweating profusely from beneath! As she finished getting herself ready, her heart was full of excitement and terror but also ached with a sense of deep sadness- knowing she may never be accepted back into this place again. She took a few extra seconds to look around her and take it all in; that one last time. The echoes and shadows of her past; as if set upon every wall, every floor space, and in every corner; conjured up around her like a projection of her former life. Some time had passed since that little girl had sat on the edge of that bed and dreamt of being loved by a handsome prince; who'd take her away on his shiny white horse and build her a beautiful cottage in the middle of a forest where their son and daughter would play endlessly in the tall grass. Life had carried her upon its fragile wings to this point in time. When finally, she could fly free, away from her birdcage, with her wings gliding the thermal breeze upon her wanderlust journey.

As usual- for this time of the morning, her mother was already sat, already busy working her meticulous hands towards the dinner service for that night. A dinner that she was destined never to taste. Her siblings were all busy, too, rushing to prepare for their day ahead and oblivious to the fact; that they may never see their sister again. All blissfully unaware of the changing hands of fate besieging them very soon. A fate, which escaped their grasp, with each second that passed and with each step she took, ever closer towards that front door and ever closer to being out in that big wide world, and as if she was leaving home; for the very first and very last time.

"Ok... Mumma, mai chalthi hoon *(Mum... I'm going)*," she said hesitantly, swallowing hard on that sudden lump of sadness in her throat.

Knowing these were possibly the very last words she'd ever say to her mother; she wanted to stop and hug her; to tell her everything and tell her how much she loved her and how sorry she was for what she was about to do. But she knew she couldn't. She couldn't say or do anything out of the ordinary or afford anything to raise any suspicions. Instead, she looked down at her reluctant feet and quietly urged them- *Go! Move! It is now or never!*

STEPS

> *"She had waited all her life for something, and it had killed her when it found her"* Zora Neale Hurston

For a moment, with her legs turning to jelly and her head suddenly dizzy, she wondered if she might faint! If she did, it would all be ruined! But thankfully, somehow, her feet carried her across her threshold and out of her home. These few steps she'd taken countless times before; felt so much more significant today. They were to change her life forever, like steppingstones toward her life's most important transition. It was as if she was being uprooted at her very soil and plunged into a new planting of adulthood, leading her onto a whole new chapter of life from which there was no going back. In an instant, she'd go from solely being- someone's daughter, sister, and property; to being a woman in her own right, and then, a wife and, one day, even a mother! Now that she knew; what it was to love, to love so desperately- that you can barely breathe without it, to love so hard that everything besides it; pales into insignificance. Stopping momentarily outside the front door; she looked back; taking a long deep breath and a quick snapshot; like a treasured final image of home.

Now or never! She commanded herself, just as Raj suddenly beeped his car horn, making her jump and rush to the passenger side.

"Time to go!" he impatiently called out.

"Yes… *Yes, it is!*" she replied knowingly before fixing her gaze on the open road ahead.

AIRFIELD

1.45 pm, fifteen minutes earlier than expected, and eager to jump on the sails of her promised new adventure, she stood, trembling uncontrollably from the biting winds, as the tiny hairs on her skin stood on end in anticipation. She now regretted not accepting Sarita's kind offer; of a second helping of her renowned hot ginger chai. Sometimes, it had been the very thing that prompted her visits there, and she couldn't help but wonder in despair; *if she would ever get to taste Sarita's wonderful chai again?* But on further contemplation, having just bare-faced lied to Sarita- about where she was going and what she was doing, the prospect of indulging her friend's hospitality any longer felt quite disrespectful and verged on grotesque!

The winds picked up, pace, alongside her quickening heartbeat, as she looked up at the impending grey skies and frantically prayed!

Please, dear God, please...! Please let him come to me! Pleeeeeease!

Tightly clenching her small handbag to her quivering chest, she tried to hold herself together as if afraid of otherwise falling apart. Her small handbag was a distinct reminder of all she had left now and all that; she had left behind. Everything which could not fit into this little bag was now estranged, both possessions and people. But in truth, she truly needed little else besides him. With no actual possessions, no money, passport, clothes, jewels, books, photos, toiletries- nothing besides her tattered old handbag; containing some loose change, her favourite pink lipstick, a handful of tissues, and her magic keyring- she was genuinely forsaking everything and everyone, just for him. He would now have to fill every voided space and prove enough to sustain her for the rest of her life. She knew this was a one-way ticket with no returns! But she also knew; that he was worth it! He was worth any sacrifice, for he was her *one* person. That twin soul, besides whom everything made more sense and with whom everything felt a little better, safer, and so much more worthwhile. He was the very reason for any season, and he was her eternal spring of hope, and beside him and besides that very hope, nothing else mattered.

Still, she had yet to learn where she was going. No idea of what was going to happen to her and when? And besides knowing that today was her Wedding Day! - everything else before her was a mystery! A giant puzzle, caught in this ruthless gamble on her life, caught on the turn of a penny or single dime and bargained on that one roll of a dice.

Please, God, please, let it be a lucky six! She prayed... flutters...

Then came an onslaught of uninvited thoughts, fleetingly terrorising her restless head. Holding her hostage inside her niggling doubts and fears, she conjured disturbing images inside her mind's eye and wondered- *What if Inder doesn't show up? What if he's changed his mind or had an accident? What if my father kills my mother? What if my family, his family, or both our families turn up, hold our feet, and beg us to stop? What if God Almighty steps in and, with a single bolt of lightning, strikes us both down to punish us for our forbidden love?*

Finally, she held her hands up at the sides of her head and tightly clasped her scalp as if trying to crush the torment away. Continuing to pace back and forth, she tried hard to focus on anything else but these endlessly terrifying- 'what *ifs!*' But even then, she still couldn't help but wonder;

...if it wasn't too late to turn back, go back to Sarita's house, and forget about this crazy plan? She could make it just before Raj's pick-up by 3 pm! And no one would be any the wiser! Should she... should she go back before it's too late?

Glancing at her wristwatch- now reading 1.52 pm, she suddenly heard the growl of an oncoming scooter, quickly followed by the crunching sounds of approaching footsteps! Her heart skipped a beat as the dust flew up from the gravelly airfield floor, and she fought against the winds blocking her view. Almost too frightened to look up, she feared who the footsteps might belong to! Once her vision cleared, she could only make out an approaching figure and a pair of highly polished shoes! Alas! It was *him! Thank God! Thank God, it is you!* Her heart cried with relief.

He reached his arms out towards her. She rushed to him and collapsed into them. Their erratic heartbeats, pounding and reverberating between their chests, finally unifying into a steady rhythm; as the world started to fall away like petals from the sides of a wilting rose-

...he loves me... he loves me not... He Loves Me!

He held her tightly, trying to calm and warm her shivering body; as it quivered like a leaf inside the canopy of his arms. Their lips met. The warmth penetrated their faces as they closed their eyes to escape the flying dust- swooning around them like a tornado of sand. They, as if the very eye of the storm. After a moment, she looked up and, through the hazy gritty horizon, could only just make out an approaching dark silhouette in the sky, followed by the squawking sound of a large black crow. It's clapping thunderous wings, startling her heartbeat again, as it hovered over their heads, circling beneath the big grey sky. Like an air raid warning, its loud caws cut through the rushing sounds of the winds. They pushed deeper into their embrace, deeper into their oblivion. Before, besides the distant sound of the crow; besides the cyclone rushes of dust and the heavily weighted sky above; they were utterly alone... alone together, but never lonely again.

He checked his watch- now 1.56 pm and scooped her into his arms to help her mount his white scooter. Forcibly holding their heads down and fighting the gusts of dusty winds, they held on for dear life; as Inder sped away. Leaving behind them; the continuing caws of the black crow and the lost cyclones of dust.

Before, gradually, everything behind them was erased, and the bike picked up its pace upon the open road. Her hair pulled away like a racehorse's mane. Her chunni scarf flew up like a shooting star, and a sudden euphoria took hold as she held her arms out and open; finally free as a bird; with her wings unclipped and spread-eagled, riding the thermal waves. She was wanderlust personified, and inside her uncorked mind, her defiant heart declared-

No one can stop us now! Not even God Almighty himself!

FUSS FREE

Twenty minutes later and they'd reached a strange house. With little time for introductions- bar quick *hellos* amongst the nervous smiles; exchanged with a couple she'd never met before; they were swiftly ushered into separate rooms. There was a distinct scent of lemons in the air; as the lady manhandled her into a small side room and pointed at the red bridal suit; laid out perfectly upon the small double bed, which dominated the space. Next to it, a clearly artificial jewellery set was placed on red satin inside a burgundy velvet box. Its scattered fake pearls, sparkling in the afternoon light, delicately set amongst the other multi-coloured gemstones, were like peaks of snow-capped mountains between a majestic rainbow. Simply seeing the bridal gown and jewellery set- such a clear image of an Indian bride! - had suddenly made her feel acutely daunted, shy, and embarrassed. As the reality- of what she was about to do; suddenly dawned on her, like a rain cloud releasing over her head and alongside the painful lump inside her throat; she fought off a sudden urge to burst out into tears.

"It's for you. Hope it's, ok?" the lady delicately enquired, smiling from the doorway, "...you don't need to be shy... not with us. This is your big day! No time for shyness now!" she chuckled, "...all will be fine... you'll see... we have all in hand... everything is organised," she tried reassuring her, and if it weren't for the slight terror in her eyes, she'd almost have convinced her!

Sudesh smiled meekly and nodded her head. As her heart raced ever faster, getting ever closer to the fruition of this-so-called meticulous plan! With her butterflies in frenzied chaos, she patiently smiled and waited; for the lovely lady to take heed and grant her some privacy.

"Oh! Sorry! Sorry! You get ready..." the lady finally clocked on as she anxiously turned to leave, "...I will be outside. Just call me if you need anything. Oh, and also, that lemonade is fresh- for you. He said- you like lemonade!" she added with another chuckle before leaving, with the door slightly ajar.

Fresh cold lemonade- just what the doctor ordered! She gulped it down, forcing the lump of tears down with it. *Lemonade...* it was always an instant reminder of him; of them; of their love affair, and in some ways; how she ended up here- right now; here, in this stranger's house, getting ready to get married! It occurred to her that, in some ways, it had all started with this simple thing... *just a cold glass of lemonade!*

DENIED

She lifted the bridal gown against her body and looked in the mirror, barely able to recognise herself. Even when she stared harder and harder, still, everything seemed unrecognisable and strange... even her own reflection. Suddenly, she was awash with such deep-seated sadness that she could no longer hold back her tears. It hit her! She was about to deny all her family, all her closest friends, and everyone she knew- this once-in-a-lifetime chance to rejoice and celebrate the most important and most auspicious day in any girl's life! Her precious mother; would be denied the opportunity to experience so many crucial wedding moments in her daughter's marriage. All the things she'd likely have spent years imagining, planning, prepping, and dreaming of. Things she'd now never get to experience or bear witness to. At least, not with this newly estranged daughter, in any case!

MISSING PIECES

Everything would have been different if the couple had married with their family's support and blessings. There'd have been months of building preparations, activities, festivities, rituals, and customs; all leading up to that big day. Kickstarted; with that first introduction, through to the engagement, and up until that final farewell- when she'd be sat inside a fully decorated Doli cart and led to her new life- right across the street! But now, all of that would be forsaken. Like pages missing from a whole storybook, where the start would jump straight to the end. Or a puzzle, where the edges and center would be formed, yet still missing the surrounding pieces- to be complete. But what else could she do? This was the sacrifice for their love. This was the heavy price; they'd have to pay, amongst any future costs- which they'd not even banked on yet! These would be the missing pages and missing puzzle pieces, forever lost. Still, she was wise enough to realise that even after all those frantic preparations had been done and dusted and even after all the rigmarole of a permitted wedding; had taken place... what else would be left beside the two of them together, as Man and Wife? The very reason for any of it, in the first place!

BRIDE ON BACK

Princess Sudesh- radiant in her bright red bridal gown. Prince Inder- the perfect gentleman, in his crisp white suit, his perfectly polished shoes, gleaming like treasure, at the foot of his mountain.

They rushed towards his white scooter (the closest they'd ever get to that full fairy tale image- of a prince taking his princess upon his white horse!) They couldn't afford to be late for their allocated time slot and miss the golden hour of opportunity! The late-afternoon rush hour traffic was already picking up pace, alongside the mounting petrol-induced smog surrounding the busy city streets- where people clamoured to snatch the final day's bargains and rushed to sell off the day's fresh produce. About to mount the scooter, dressed in their full bridal attire- they both stopped momentarily and looked at one another. Having never seen one another dressed like this before and feeling giddy and overwhelmed, they instinctively burst out into fits of laughter! What a complete spectacle- they looked! They could barely believe their eyes- seeing how they were dressed on an otherwise regular Friday afternoon! Then, simply contemplating what they were about to do, made them even more hysterical! They laughed and laughed! Their laughter stemmed from a myriad of emotions; relief, anxiety, nerves, exhilaration, and excitement, alongside the sheer ludicrously of it all, indeed not escaping them! They laughed until their tears came fourth, and then, having clocked the time on his wristwatch, Inder quickly composed himself and kick-started his scooter.

Taking long, drawn-out breaths, they both tried to find calm whilst still intermittently overcome with their childish giggles— the ones they once had as kids over the most benign and silly things. The ones when you were most expected to be serious and adult-like but couldn't resist laughing! And just like back then, no sooner had one found composure than the other would set them off again! The vibration of their laughter, shaking between their bodies and only making matters worse! But what else could they do now- but laugh? It was either laugh or cry! And they certainly had no time to cry! Laughing sure did help! Just like when they were kids, it took the sting out of the bite, helped them cope with awkward situations, and somehow diminished the gravity of everything. Alongside their puppy-like frantic excitement, it was always this very laughter; which had bonded and grounded them.

Once they'd finally stopped laughing, they were mutually overcome with a renewed steely determination, and with a glint in their eyes, they sped off down the open road like wildfire shouting devastation through the trees-

'*Fuck Yeah!*'

CLIMAX

Although the sight of a young virile man dressed in his Sunday bests and riding upon a white scooter with a ready-made bride on his back had often been depicted in Bollywood movies- it was still quite a surprising sight on the dusty streets of New Delhi! But they'd come too far now to care about the spectacle they made. Just like in those classic Bollywood movies- the hero was finally escaping with his would-be bride, after much trial and tribulation, had been picked against their love.

In the film, their adversaries would right now be reeling, aghast in defeat as the martyrs of love escape their grasp. Accompanying the action would be a piercingly high-pitched lover's theme tune- serenading the revolt and intensely building the suspense sequence with highly charged emotions and evocative monologues, leading the audiences searingly towards the movie's climax. When inevitably, the ill-fated couple, along with their scooter, would tragically go flying off the edge of a cliff- indicative of a joint-lovers suicide. Or else be shot dead and die in one another's arms while declaring their undying love and hoping to be reunited in that promised heaven. When finally, their souls would transcend to Moksha *(Emancipation)*.

And so would be complete; the orchestrated mass manipulation of its loyal viewing public! A sanctimoniously indoctrinating society, returning its faithful to the expected virtues and morality codes; in line with religion, tradition, and honour. Through the clever use of fear mongering, crowd pleasing and crowd control, we are reminded that we are merely victims of a predestined fate, caught inside a perpetually inescapable cycle of karma and forever at the mercy of often vengeful Gods. The inevitable doomed demise of forbidden love, forewarning other rebel hearts- ethered by the populous; to tread cautiously! Often funded by deep-pocketed corrupt politicians, business Moghuls, and staunch religious community leaders; these movies hold hidden agendas for these puppeteers; who exorcise subliminal power and control over the populous and the narrative and remind us of the confines of traditional piety, virtue, and respect. So that; even while ensuring we are spellbound and hypnotized by the beautiful stars, sumptuous song sequences, sublime scenery shooting, and generic story formulas and lulled into a false sense of security and even whilst we fervently root for the star-crossed lovers; we are too, being simultaneously drip-fed- how breaking the rules, ousting religion, tradition, and honour, will never go unpunished. And although on the surface, it may appear as if true love had prevailed against all the odds- it was only ever inconsequentially won and claimed via the predicted and prophesied demise of that very love and the need for the lovers, in the end, to die! Thus, forbidden love was never openly permissible for indulgence, never achieved without retribution and reckoning, if it is fatefully born on this pre-claimed, righteous brigaded people's holy earth!

But in real life, neither knew how this love story would end! Whether they must die or be killed off- just to be together? In truth, all they had was this very precise moment in time, a seemingly meticulous plan, and their deeply exhilarating desires, hopes, and dreams- all of which were slowly melting away like snowflakes alongside the setting of the sun.

SPECTACLE

While waiting at a red light, she could feel the many prying eyes glaring at them as if they were aliens from another planet! - that discerning grin of that wrinkly old man, aged like a prune in the sun and sat manspreading inside his tinseled tuk-tuk, surrounded by effigies of his Hindu God's, like bodyguards protecting him from the hazardous and treacherous city streets.

Then, that wonderous curiosity; emanating from the innocently confused angel-faced girl; crossing the footpath in her broken sandals, with her greasy hair matted onto her dirty scalp, tightly holding onto her empty begging pot, and wondering if she was dreaming a fairy-tale to life?

Then, the flummoxed and astounded expression on the clown-like-made-up face of that gilded golden lady; sat inside her air-conditioned-chauffeur driven car, sneering down her Gucci spectacles, with a yearning nostalgia, as well as an affronted disdain, for the brazen rebellion of these escaped lovers!

"...Penji! *(Sister!)* Oh, Maaa! *(Oh, mother!)* You will never guess what I saw today- driving on the Akbar Road...!?" she'd no doubt spew her gossip for her kitty party guests that night!

Then, just as the precious green light appeared, she leaned closer to Inder and embraced him even tighter. Momentarily closing her eyes to block out all the many questioning and judging faces, repugnant stares, and pointless noise surrounding them. Inder revved his engine louder, roaring like a lion on a hunter's path, as the dust blew up from the city streets; into veils of clouds and obscured the lovers out of sight.

MISSING GIRL

When she opened her eyes again, she noticed his wristwatch reading 3 pm. Her breath caught in her throat; she suddenly realised that mayhem would be transcending upon her family at this precise moment in time! - having only just discovered the fact that Sudesh was missing! Soon, a desperate and frantic search would ensue- starting first with her friend's houses, before a select few trusted family friends would be discretely summoned to help track down the missing girl! Like sleuth detectives dissecting her last movements, they'd debate all the possibilities, trying to solve the mystery of her disappearance. Before long, it would dawn on them; that the girl was not just missing; but had, in fact, *run away!* Worst still, with her *forbidden lover!*

With the younger females calling for calm, the others would no doubt be caught up in a catastrophising panic, suddenly unable to function. Like her mother, whom she could imagine; falling to the floor and crying out to the heavens for mercy, begging *all her Gods for help!* Then would start all the finger-pointing; '...who was to blame for this girl gone wild? Whose fault was it that she'd gone AWOL? Who had failed in their responsibilities- towards this now, fallen girl?'

Undoubtedly, all the blame would befall her poor mother's shoulders! Always the one, who got blamed for everything, and now, thanks to Sudesh, left with another boulder of weight upon her already heavy soul! But they'd all agree on one thing; '...that somehow, they'd get that belligerent runaway girl back home, where she belonged, before anyone else found out and before it was too late, and she was forever forsaken!'

And so would start a maddening pursuit for damage limitation, knowing- once they'd got their hands on her- *there'd be hell to pay!*

They'd need to make an example of her, to warn off other naïve and stupid girls and ensure no one else ever escaped or dared raise their eyes above the parapet, look beyond their threshold, or entertain such crazy thoughts and dream such treacherous dreams, ever again!

NIGHT FLIES

As the scooter whizzed faster down the open, welcoming stretch of road, her tears, too, pulled away from her face with the razor-sharp winds, and her long dark hair was caught beneath her sparkling red chunni-scarf as if at the mercy of the rampant breeze's final dance. Lit inside the twinkling sunset, it shimmered and sparkled like fireflies in emancipation. She held her chunni tightly to her head, praying; the entire packet of 30 Kirby grips proved strong enough to keep it from flying onto an unsuspected windscreen behind her!

16

STITCHED UP

"Whatever our souls are made of, his and mine are the same" Emily Bronte, 'Wuthering Heights'

NUPTIAL

Luckily, they arrived just in time at the Hindu temple near Canard Place. Surprisingly, Inder had invited just over one hundred guests! Mainly consisting of his co-workers from the All-India Radio Station; the faces present- were clearly from his side alone, and not a single familiar face from her own. Suddenly struck with imposter syndrome, it felt like she was attending someone else's wedding! Yet, knowing that it couldn't have been easy, organising a wedding at such short notice and keeping it a secret from Inder's father- who shared many of the same co-workers; she realised that even in the absence of her own loved ones, it was indeed a commendable feat! Walking in further, it was soon apparent; that this would not be the quiet and intimate secret runaway wedding she'd expected it to be. Instead, it appeared like an entirely above board, legitimate marriage, with a beautifully decorated hall, finely dressed guests, a real wedding Mandap *(a structure erected for a Hindu fire ceremony)*, and a bonafide holy priest! And even though all the guests seemed privy to the fact this was a secret runaway wedding- being held against their respective parent's wishes; they'd still all turned up, dressed to the nines and sharing the same contagious strength and courage, rooting for the couple in an enchanted rebellion. Indeed, it was a room filled with their tribe of rebel hearts and lovers of love!

Walking down the long corridor, eager guests intermittently greeted them as if they were mini celebrities! The moist faces watching them in awe; seemed to share a similarly strange expression; both a mixture of nervous enthusiasm, slight terror, and a little helping of pity! Inder hurriedly repeated, name after name, in an almost quick-fire round, as he tried earnestly to appear- cool as a cucumber. Even if his tightening grip, beads of sweat on his brows, and rushed stutters; suggested otherwise! Her ears had long since stopped listening to all the names being hollered at her as she struggled to hear anything beyond the sound of her pounding heartbeat- which resembled her father's thudding footsteps, as if marching between her ears! Her mind quickly wandered off- far from her pasted-on quivering smile; as she started to imagine- calamity after calamity, like a pick and mix of horror movie clips, sequentially building up to a crescendo of tribulation. With her blood pressure rising inside the havoc of her mind, somehow, she responded gracefully, nodding and smiling on cue at the many faces thrust before her.

Once inside, she almost gasped aloud at how beautiful it all looked. The finely decorated hall, complete with flowers and lights, was like a thing of fairytales! But the mounting pressure cooker inside, almost ready to blow from her nerves, still seemed to command her attention! Seemingly, getting worse; with each step, she took closer and closer towards what felt like imminent danger. Besides this, the endlessly forced awkward hugs with strangers; were becoming tiresome and only served to loosen the Kirby grips even further, now annoyingly poking into her scalp! With her head drooped down beneath her chunni scarf, she struggled to peer beyond its shimmering edge and only just spotted a handful of sweaty alarm-clicking faces, whose pasted-on smiles looked as if they were disguising a ticking time bomb, in her midst! Then, as her moist palm started to slip away from Inder's grip, she sensed; that he was becoming calmer and calmer in his resolve as if he'd escaped a storm and had almost reached his final goal. At the same time, she felt the very opposite. Like she was being whipped up even further into a frenzy the closer she got to the very eye of the storm! The parting crowds, appearing as if deceptively leading her towards the gates of hell, ready to take in the sacrifice of her forsaken soul!

UNINVITED GUEST

Stopping dead in his tracks, he suddenly yanked at her hand, instantly bringing her wandering mind back down to earth! She looked at him, confused, as he forcibly pulled her away with him and led her into an inconspicuous space between two pillars, aligning the red-carpeted path. She could sense something had shaken him up. The sudden change in his demeanour and the colour quickly falling from his face, indicating that something was terribly wrong!

"What? What is it?" She anxiously asked.

His widened eyeballs scared her as he quickly checked behind her and apprehensively peered- repeatedly, from the side of the pillar, before finally turning to her as white as a sheet.

"O.k.!" He said assertively.

But she knew the sound of that *O.k.* was anything, but...!

"You must promise me... you will not panic!" he continued.

Of course, this immediately had the opposite effect- putting her into an instant panic!

"Oh no! What? Oh God! What? What is it?"

"My... my father is here!"

"No! Oh no! Oh God... It's all over!" She tried pulling away, shaking her head in disbelief just before he pulled her back in again.

"Stop! Look!... Don't worry!... I think I spotted him- first! He's still waiting at the front! He's not seen us yet! Thinks- we are not here yet!" he continued, anxiously realising- "Shit! Shit! Somebody must have told him! Dammit! Dammit!" He paced back and forth in front of her, trying desperately to think. Then, suddenly stopping and realising- he needed to get a grip, he looked at her intently,

"O.k.!... O.k...! It is O.k.!" he breathed deeply, "I need to ask you for sure now- for the last time... as it could be... I mean, it is possible that even...your family is here!"

"No! No! No...!" She shuddered as tears instantly fell from her heavily mascaraed eyes and traced ink pathways down her flushed cheeks.

"Tell me one thing... are you one hundred percent sure- this is definitely what you want? You will not change your mind? Are you ready for this?"

Feeling faint and overcome with emotion- if it hadn't been for the adrenaline pumping through her veins like lightning, she'd have collapsed! But she knew in her heart- what she wanted... It was him, and *only him!* She took a deep breath and looked at him- dead in his eyes and nodded.

"Ok...ok...!" he smiled nervously, "Now or never, meri jaan! *(My love!)*"

"Now or never!" she defiantly agreed.

MANDAP

They hurtled towards the hall's back entrance and headed straight towards the beautifully prepared Mandap *(wedding altar)*. Like a mirage in the desert, it appeared beyond the parted sea of people, with its floral pillars, which stood like an enchanted gateway into a secret utopia. Struggling to stay upright, she leaned down, pulling at Inder's arm as he practically dragged her in with him. She could see the image of a frail old priest standing proudly at the entrance of the alter- bare-chested, with his sun-kissed skin wrinkled beneath his vast array of holy beads, and wearing nothing, but a humble saffron dhoti *(robe)*, precariously wrapped around his manhood. His wide eager smile, almost startling, as he waited there, like a checking-in agent at the gates of a nirvana paradise. He stood, exuding both authority and service; only once they'd reached him, he stepped towards them, looking almost ecstatic- as if maybe; he, too, was a secret rebel heart beneath his pious cloth! Or perhaps, he, too, was taken up in the mass hysteria of this most impetus day and most scandalous marriage. Everyone there seemed to be sailing on the wings of this adolescent revolt and proclamation of true love. Before he could

STITCHED UP SUE!

instigate any formalities or pleasantries, Inder stopped him in his tracks, abruptly glaring at him and sharply waving his hand as if indicating- that time was of the essence! Sensing this urgency, the priest nervously nodded- already privy to the high stakes of this secret runaway wedding- for which he'd already negotiated a heavily doubled fee! Also, intent on pursuing this money train to its final destination, he assertively turned towards the fire pit and signalled for the couple to follow him before anyone could derail it. Frantically muttering his prayers while holding tightly to his tattered prayer book and waving it between his leathery shrivelled hands, he exhaled a plethora of chants as Sudesh picked up on his sickly garlic-ridden breath. Discretely pulling her face away, she looked down and noticed the priest's filthy blackened feet alongside his long gnarly fungal-ridden toenails! - gripping the ground beneath, as if he, too, felt that same fear of being ripped away from his current spot; he seemed consumed with mutual desperation to complete the rites of this marriage. Pushing on, as quickly as humanly possible, before any uninvited guest- could come and put a stop to things, at times, he was barely audible. Ruthlessly skipping any unnecessary rigmarole and mantras- as he fast-tracked the service in an almost comical fashion; the palpable tension was plucked out of the air as each mantra passed from his profusely perspiring lips.

BLOOD BROTHER

"Kanya ka bhai? *(Brother of the bride?)*." The priest suddenly blurted, sending the entire congregation into a communal panic and harshly reminding them of one of the many unforeseen ramifications- of a runaway marriage!

Thankfully, the ever-resourceful Inder had already planned for this eventuality. He confidently turned to his close friend Mr. Chibber, beckoning him forthwith to perform the rite, traditionally befallen to blood brothers of the bride. Although Sudesh's heart sank, realising this was yet another honouree task of her marriage, being denied to her actual blood relatives; she had to accept it was all part of their sacrifice.

No matter how sad she felt about it, once she'd witnessed how graciously and respectfully, Mr. Chibber obliged, she felt both flattered and grateful. Indeed, all Inder's many friends had stepped up for the sake of these two star-struck lovers, and like them; they too were willing to forgo tradition and formalities and, just for today, throw caution to the wind!

DONE DEED

Hidden behind the crowd- the secret marriage ceremony was back on track. Inder's father's silhouette- barely visible; as the risky proceedings continued and as he stood blissfully unaware; his eldest son's marriage ceremony had not only commenced but was almost finished! Little idea of the treachery taking place right under his nose; he was gobsmacked when the couple suddenly walked through the congregation and straight up to him! Looking at them, dumbfounded and confused; for a moment, he seemed oblivious to the fact that the couple were married! Still stood defiantly, glaring at them, with an almost smug expression- he seemed to have assumed; that he'd gotten there in time and could still stop proceedings. But then, after suddenly noticing the couple's tightly clasped hands, flower garlands hanging off their necks, red tikkas- in the middle of their foreheads, and most significantly- the red Sindhoor *(vermillion cosmetic powder)* etched across Sudesh's hair parting- it suddenly, dawned on him, like a shot to his head... they were already *Married!* He'd not only failed to stop them from entering the venue but failed to stop the wedding altogether, and now, it was clear as day- they were officially Husband & Wife, and there was not a single thing he could do about it!

OBJECTION OVER-RULED!

Inder could see the anger building up inside his father's eyes as the penny finally dropped! Sudesh dared not even look up at her now- officially designated father-in-law! Although she could feel his piercing eyes, almost burning a hole into her, she continued to look straight down at his sandaled feet. Sighing deeply in disbelief, his father shook his head vigorously as if that alone could somehow undo all that was done. Inder stepped forward confidently, holding his new brides' hand, as she strangely noted- just how much bigger his feet looked; compared with his father's! - Her attention on such trivial and insignificant things; was always like a subconscious coping mechanism, built inside her since she was a child.

"Well, you are here now, Daddy ji..." He spoke with newfound confidence, "...You may as well- give us your blessing? It is done! There is nothing left for you to refuse or stop!"

Assertively pulling Sudesh down with him, Inder tried to touch his father's feet to receive their first marriage blessing (An Indian tradition, showing a significant mark of respect for elders; who touch the bowing heads and pass on ancestral-bound blessings) But his dad, rather insultingly, stepped away;

leaving them both touching the dusty floor, instead. Furious, he tried feebly to retaliate, retreating, and stepping back like a cobra recoiling from its prey- knowing that an immediate attack was futile.

"I vill go! ...I vill report this illegal vedding! Right now- to poolis!" He shouted so loud; that he made Sudesh flinch and caught everyone's attention around them.

His father had assumed that Sudesh was still 20 years old- thus, not legally permitted to marry without her parent's consent. But unbeknownst to him, she'd already turned 21 days before and now, by law- was allowed to marry whomever she wished without anyone's consent.

"Daddy ji!... You can report us- all you want! But the fact remains- we are married, by law now! And even if the police arrest us, they cannot do anything! And you should know- after such action- my relationship with you and all of my family- will be finished... over!"

"It is! ...all already over!!!" Inder's father roared, with such a loud and trembling force, that his explosive presence almost shook the floor beneath them!

Finally, Sudesh found the courage to glance up at him momentarily, catching a slight glimpse of his flushed red face, full of putrid anger. Yet he also seemed undeniably sad, within his silent defeat, looking away in disgust and shaking his head wearily before he staunchly marched away, with his crunching sandals instantly reminding her of her father!

FINAL STITCH

"Perhaps it was freedom itself that choked her"
Patricia Highsmith

Sighing deeply with relief, they finally embraced. She desperately fought an urge to cry aloud without holding back anything. That desperate want to let it all go and relinquish all, which had built up inside her like a ferocious volcano over the past few months, weeks, and days. She yearned for that cathartic release from all those heavily pent-up and burdening emotions. That frantic fear, worry, anxiety, nervousness, stress, anguish, pain, despair, and confusion consumed her soul and beseeched them both; from the first moment they'd fallen in love, it had felt like being engulfed inside a supernova! Sensing her desperate need, he held her ever tightly.

"Bus... bus... bus... meri jaan... *(Enough... enough... enough... my love...)* It is ok. It is done." His mellifluous and velvet voice calmly washed over her and steadied her eruption. He held her until her heartbeat fell into a peaceful rhythm beside his.

HOPE SPRINGS ETERNAL...

"...And with the purest threads of love, they were finally stitched together. Their torn souls restitched, and their wanton hearts repaired, to form a strong new fabric"

As the congregation hastily congratulated the tepidly happy couple, they all made their way to a local restaurant for a foray- booked by Inder's friends as a wedding gift. Quietly sensitive, the celebrations rightfully forsook any need for extravagance, overt displays of excessiveness and indulgence, and proved to be a notably restrained affair. All present; keenly mindful of being respectful and inoffensive; by avoiding getting too carried away or too drunk; were unified in their poise and grace. A calm celebration of joy commenced after such an exhausting and tumultuous day- which had preceded it!

Nonetheless, all the obligatory requirements of such an occasion had been carefully ticked off to mark this memorable day, including a modest D.J. set-up, a simple wedding cake, some tasteful decorations, and a simple no-frills meal served during the couple's first dance.

"Please all put your hands together for the newlyweds- *Mr. & Mrs. Inderpal Wilku!"* The D.J. triumphantly called!

And hearing that, for the very first time, followed by such a magnanimous cheer, was like the sweetest icing upon their single- tier cake. Their favourite song- 'Jalte Hai Jiske Liye Teri Aankhon Ke Diye' *(For whom the lamps of your eyes are burning)*, blared from the speakers. The crowd swelled into a closed circle around them with hopeful eyes. And they knew at once; they'd found their tribe. And as they held hands and locked eyes, they also knew that so long as they continued to see their own reflection- staring right back; they'd always be filled with this same mesmerising serenity.

She- forever his sweet biscuit, and he- forever, her cool lemonade.

THE END.

But only for now, as every ending heralds the **start,** of a new beginning...

Volume 2 -

RIPPED UP SUE

coming soon!

Printed in Great Britain
by Amazon